AME

Is My

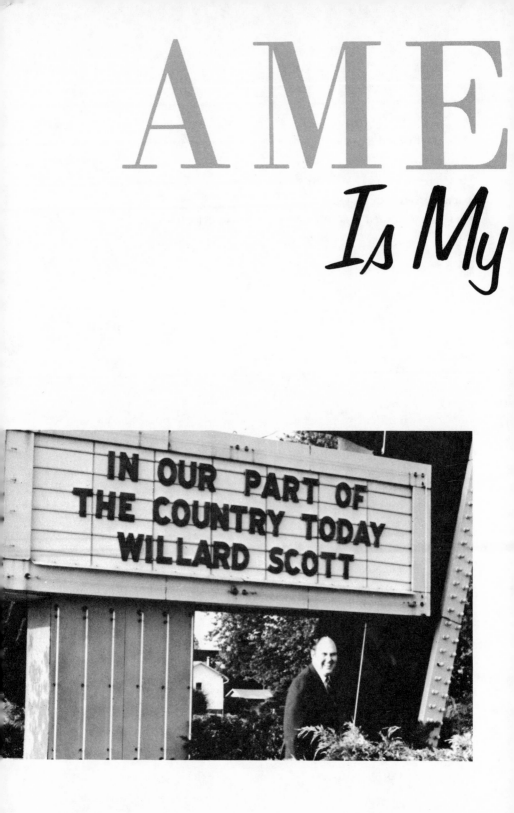

IN OUR PART OF
THE COUNTRY TODAY
WILLARD SCOTT

RICA

Neighborhood

by Willard Scott

WITH DANIEL PAISNER

SIMON AND SCHUSTER

New York London Toronto Sydney Tokyo

COPYRIGHT © 1987 BY MARIAH ENTERPRISES
ALL RIGHTS RESERVED
INCLUDING THE RIGHT OF REPRODUCTION
IN WHOLE OR IN PART IN ANY FORM.
PUBLISHED BY SIMON AND SCHUSTER
A DIVISION OF SIMON & SCHUSTER, INC.
SIMON & SCHUSTER BUILDING
ROCKEFELLER CENTER
1230 AVENUE OF THE AMERICAS
NEW YORK, NY 10020
SIMON AND SCHUSTER AND COLOPHON ARE REGISTERED TRADEMARKS OF
SIMON & SCHUSTER, INC.
DESIGNED BY KAROLINA HARRIS
MANUFACTURED IN THE UNITED STATES OF AMERICA
10 9 8 7 6 5 4 3 2 1
LIBRARY OF CONGRESS CATALOGING IN PUBLICATION DATA
SCOTT, WILLARD.
   AMERICA IS MY NEIGHBORHOOD.

   1. UNITED STATES—BIOGRAPHY. 2. UNITED STATES—
DESCRIPTION AND TRAVEL—1981- . 3. SCOTT, WILLARD—
JOURNEYS—UNITED STATES. 4. SCOTT, WILLARD—FRIENDS
AND ASSOCIATES. I. PAISNER, DANIEL. II. TITLE.
CT220.S35 1987   920'.073   87-14550
ISBN 0-671-62585-3

Acknowledgments

This book could not have been written without the extra efforts of Barbara Gess, Cathy Hemming, and Joni Evans at Simon & Schuster; Jim Griffin and Dan Strone at the William Morris Agency; and the kind folks at NBC affiliate stations across the country, who opened doors and put us back in touch with many of the wonderful people you'll meet here. Also, an appreciative tip of the hat to two great American institutions: NBC and the "Today" show. They've punched my ticket for all these years, and I'm grateful. And, of course, a special thanks to all of my neighbors, within these pages and without; they make my world a special place to live, rain or shine.

To three of my favorite people—
Nancy Fields, Morrison Krus, and
Millicent Thomas. Without them,
taking care of business would be an
impossible chore; with them, it's a
sunny delight. I cherish their
support and devotion.

Contents

Contents

Contents

America Is My Neighborhood

I'm always in my element.

1 It's a Wonderful Life

It was July. It was 6:35 A.M., Central Daylight Time. And while most everybody else in this great country of ours was in bed, dreaming about a day at the beach, I was standing in snow at an elevation approaching twelve thousand feet. I was in a place they call the Wausatch Mountains just outside of Salt Lake City, near a ski resort called Snowbird. It was thirty-eight degrees. With me were the governor of the state of Utah, handfuls of local politicians, and assorted members of the area chambers of commerce. There are always extras —it's the closest I'll ever come to having an entourage of my very own—and on this brisk summer morning there were some two hundred of them, all looking pretty much as tired and cold and miserable as you could get. But not me. I was cold, I'll admit, and I could have used a couple of winks more, but I was pumped up and working, and I was having the time of my life.

Most of us had been up since four. It took a while to move all of us, and the broadcasting equipment from Salt Lake City's NBC affiliate KINS-TV, from the sleeping city and up the mountain by aerial tram. The KINS crew, many of them at the tail end of their working day, had their cameras pointed at me, and the satellite system used to transmit remote telecasts such as this one—the uplink—was all in place. Everyone had a job to do in that unlikeliest of places, and mine was to sit and wait. The unit manager was on the phone to New York, holding for the cue that would start me talking, that would send my words from that mountaintop, twenty-two thousand miles up to a stationary satellite, back down another twenty-two thousand miles to the Studio B control room in the RCA building in New York's Rockefeller Center, and then back out again to approximately 10 million people in every corner of these United States and, over Armed Forces Television, to Canada, Australia, West Germany, and anywhere else you might find a transplanted American or two.

A voice in New York whispered my cue across a good chunk of the country and into the headset of my unit manager, who then pointed a finger at me to let me know we were on. At long last, my cue. Just then, with a bar of soap in hand, I made my proclamation: "We'll be right back with more of the "Today" show after this word from Safeguard, the deodorant soap with more protection and more rich lather than any other deodorant soap." In his wildest dreams, when he first looked down on that beautiful and fertile Wausatch valley and proclaimed that this was indeed the place, Brigham Young could never have envisioned an event such as this. And yet such as this is the stuff of my every working day. It is the world in which I live and work. This is my America, my backyard.

America is my office, and let me tell you, it's a pretty nice place to work. For the past seven years I have looked outside

America's window to see what the weather was doing and to pass what I see on to the many millions of television viewers who get their morning dose of news and information from NBC. On the average of about once a week I do my weather broadcast from outside the network's Rockefeller Center studios, sometimes from the streets of New York City, but usually from another part of the country entirely. In the television business we call these on-location broadcasts "remotes," and since I've been on the "Today" show I've done several hundred of them, from Rome to Rio to Roanoke.

With the help of my technical crew I've brought the sights and sounds of this country into millions of American living rooms (and more than likely, in the case of morning television, into a few bedrooms, too) from coast to coast. I've even forecasted the weather from under the midnight sun of Alaska's Mount McKinley, which the Indians reverently refer to as "the Great One."

And, in addition to my weathercasting chores at NBC (and no doubt because of them), I have been invited to countless parades and fairs, in the remotest corners of this vast country, asked to make speeches or personal appearances at store openings or civic group dinners or retirement homes, urged to attend this function and that and just to be Willard Scott. (I'm getting pretty good at this last part, let me tell you.) All told, I have made working visits to nearly one thousand American cities and towns, putting other frequent flyers to shame, and each and every one of these working visits has been a pure and absolute pleasure. I have crossed the Great Divide more times than Lewis and Clark. I have been on the Sante Fe, the Chisolm, and the Oregon trails. I ate mountain oysters and danced with Miss Kitty at the Long Branch saloon in Dodge City, Kansas. I've eaten coho salmon from the rejuvenated Lake Erie, enjoyed beignets and chicory coffee at the Cafe Dumond on the banks of the Mississippi River. I've played Santa Claus at the White House, drunk homemade corn whiskey in Kingsport, Tennessee, kissed a bear and played a clown with the Ringling Bros. Circus in Venice, Florida. I've attended Easter sunrise services in the desert outside Phoenix, Arizona. Once I even persuaded Defense Secretary Caspar Weinberger to put on a T-shirt that said,

"Buy U.S. Savings Bonds," while standing in the courtyard at the Pentagon. It's been, and it continues to be, a wonderful life.

There is such a thing as a free lunch in this country, and I've had the pleasure of more than I care to count. (No wisecracks, please.) But with all the free meals, the travel, the new places, by far the most rewarding part of who I am and what I have done are the people I've met along the way. I am blessed in that my days are filled with an ever-changing sea of strange and wonderful faces, and behind each face there lies a strange, wonderful, and uniquely American story. And boy, do I love these stories! I am and always have been a people person—a true extrovert, if you please. I am into ancestor worship and role models and all sorts of that fun stuff, and I've had a chance to do my thing with some of the grandest people on this earth. The real people of this wonderful country have added to and enriched my life, and they have convinced me more than ever before that the strength of America lies in the diversity of her population, in her people.

So you see that this great country of ours is much more than one sprawling landscape of an office (with one breathtaking view, I might add). It is also my neighborhood, it says as much right on the cover of this book, and in any truly great neighborhood you're bound to come upon bunches of truly great neighbors. This is a book about America's people, my neighbors, the plain folk like you and me who live and work in my office, in my American neighborhood. Their stories are of the sort you might hear spun over a backyard fence or at a potluck community supper. I doubt very seriously that Herman Wouk or James Michener or even Jackie Collins will be run out of the book business because of this accounting. They can rest easily. This is just a bunch of little old stories about the some of the people I've bumped into along the way. The folks you'll meet here come from places with typically American-sounding names like Stone Mountain, Georgia, or Cave Creek, Arizona, and from middle-American, Indian-sounding towns like Mishawaka, Indiana, and Neodesha, Kansas. Yes, places like these still exist, and the people you'll find there are good and decent and interesting as all get out.

These pages are filled with people positively brimming with all sorts of the right stuff, from Bethesda to Buffalo, Bismarck to Brooklyn. Together, these tiny snapshots form a broader portrait of the real folks who people our American landscape. The individuals you'll meet here have played a big part in my life, and after you've visited them with me, I'm sure they'll play a big part in yours.

So let's get on with the show. . . .

People sure do the darnedest things!

2 National Pastimes

SOME of my neighbors are hard hit by trivial pursuits, and that's as good a place to start as any. They collect Civil War relics, the folks next door, or old railroad cars (full-sized and not pint-sized), or four-fingered baseball gloves. They've strung together enough paper clips to stretch cross-country, or they've amassed the world's largest ball of twine. On every trip, my neighbors just crawl out of the woodwork to strut their unusual stuff, to show and tell, and my eyes pop out at some of the things these people do, some of the ways they've chosen to fill their attics.

Of course, there are those whose hobbies and pastimes speak to something much larger than a big ball of twine, folks who've put their head and heart and sweat into the great and good things that help to define their communities. These are the folks who've got a bead on the heartbeat of America, the ones who get off on the simple pleasures that make this country such a great place to live.

For me, well, my extracurricular activities might coax a yawn out of a few of you, but not much else. Take a microphone out of my hands and I'm just plain folks. I collect a few odds and ends in my spare moments (mostly odds), spend some quality time with my family and friends, take in an old movie, work on my Virginia farm, sip a little at a good bottle of bourbon, and watch the sun set. That's the good life, my good life. So much for my little blurb on what keeps me ticking when I'm not punching the clock.

But oh, can my ticker get excited at some of the pure and simple pleasures served up by some of my wonderfully talented neighbors! Here's a for-instance: To me, there's nothing more exciting, or more typically American, than cheerleaders and marching bands, and I could die a happy man if I knew a corps of each would be on hand at my funeral. Really, I turn to apple pie inside thinking about a halftime show on a crisp fall afternoon; forgive me, but it just turns me all red, white, and blue with excitement.

I'm an old softie for that kind of thing, and because of my passion for all that is typically American, I've been lucky enough to meet and befriend the leading innovators in both these homegrown art forms—a nationally honored leader of cheerleaders and a marching band director with more raw rah-rah to him than you can shake a baton at. You'll meet them here. You'll also meet a good friend who keeps a helicopter and a team of prizewinning horses in his backyard, and two lovely ladies who've turned on a childhood friendship to build a captivating public collection of teensy-weensy wonders.

Listen to the spirit that moves these outstanding people, the spirit that's made a heap of difference in each of their communities. It's folks like them who make this country tick and hum.

★ ★

The Hanover Area Cheerleaders strut their stuff in a special cheer they wrote for me.

"SIS-BOOM-BAH!"

★ **PAMELA AREGOOD AGNEW**

Wilkes-Barre, Pennsylvania

I don't know about you, but cheerleaders still give me goosebumps. Rah-rah-rass, kick 'em in the other knee, and all that. Seriously, I get these patriotic chills every time I see pigtails and pom-poms. Every time I see cheerleaders in action, live or on television, I'm taken back to my own high school days. I'm a kid again, full of pep and vinegar and wide-eyed enthusiasm. And when you talk about really good cheerleading—I'm talking world-class precision, here— well, that's the stuff that really gets me charged up.

Pamela Aregood Agnew really gets me charged up. And lately, in cheerleading circles and in and around Wilkes-Barre, Pennsylvania, she's been getting everybody excited. For the past two years she has coached twelve high school girls in the Hanover schools system in Wilkes-Barre to the Super Bowl of high school cheerleading—the United States Cheerleading Association National Grand Championships, in Lansing, Michigan—and this year her girls have also been named world international champs, to complement their national honors.

Not too shabby. But for all the pomp and circumstance, you can't really appreciate what these girls have done until they strut their stuff for you in person. And for me, lucky me, they pulled out all the stops in a special cheer they'd written the last time I passed through town:

Hey, everybody!
Check him out!
Willard Scott,
Knows what the weather's about!
From north to south,
From east to west,
Willard Scott,
Willard Scott,
Willard Scott,
The very best!
Yes!

Boy, Pam and her girls sure know how to make a guy feel right at home! And all of this done to a series of flips and leaps and splits that were enough to make an old guy like me cringe with envy and wonder. Imagine what would happen if you mixed the Radio City Rockettes with the June Taylor Dancers and a dozen Mary Lou Rettons, and you'll have a clearer picture of what Pam's squad can do and how well they can do it. You just can't do justice to their talents on the printed page, but trust me, these girls know what they're doing. And the reason they know what they're doing is Pamela Aregood Agnew.

"The national championships were a very big deal for me," admits Pam, who was herself a cheerleader for the Hanover Hawkeyes ten years ago and has been coaching the team since her high school graduation. "Cheerleading isn't as big here as it is in the Midwest or the South," she says during takes of our "Today" show remote, "but I think our success has revived some of the old interest. People are really coming out to see us, and the whole community has been giving their support. Lately it's been a big deal here because of the national championships and all of the attention, but I hope we're putting some of the basic excitement back into cheerleading. I hope people care about what we do not because we win awards, but because they enjoy it, because they appreciate it."

I hope so, too, because the girls on the Hanover squad deserve it. Pam runs her girls like a drill team. During the season, which runs pretty much from April to April, the girls work out anywhere from four to six hours a day. (I know people at NBC who put in a shorter day than that!) They attend a summer cheerleading camp to train for the national competitions, which are held in August. From there they move into the Hawkeye football season, and then on into basketball and wrestling. No rest for the weary on Pam's squad, and no room for the girls who can't live up to Pam's exacting standards.

"I look for a good attitude in my girls," Pam says of her rigorous selection process. "Of course, the abilities are important. You do need to be, you know, peppy, sunny, cutesy, and you do need to have the gymnastic ability. You do need good arm coordination. But you can teach some of those things. You can't teach a good attitude."

A good attitude, in Pam's estimation, also includes the ability to maintain good grades and to say no to drinking and drugs. "Cheerleaders should be role models to the rest of the school," Pam says, which is why any girl even seen smoking a cigarette in uniform will be kicked off the team. I like Pam's hard line here. In fact, Pam won't abide cigarette smoking at all, in uniform or out. "If I see a girl smoking, I don't care if she's out to dinner with her family, that's it," she says. "Maybe that's too strict, too severe, but it's the only way I know to teach the kids that cigarette smoking is stupid, it's bad for them. I think it's part of my job to protect them from things like that." I think it says something about Pam's leadership and her ability to instill good values and common sense in her charges that not one girl has strayed from this hard line in her ten years as cheerleading coach. Let's hope a few more authority figures charged with shaping the lives of our young people follow her lead.

The good folks at United Way got wind of Pam's no-nonsense attitude toward kids and drugs, and they asked her squad to develop an antidrug cheer to help stop drug abuse before it had a chance to start. The Hawkeye cheerleaders recently hosted squad captains from high schools all over the region and taught them the cheer so they could bring it back to their schools and continue the campaign there. To my mind, this is one of the simplest and most effective ways to curb drug abuse among our children; it's a real grass-roots campaign that hits home because it starts at home. It has an impact with kids because it starts with kids. The cheer goes something like this (actually it goes exactly like this, although it loses something in the translation from whoops and flips and claps to print):

> Give 'em up!
> 'Cause drugs can't win!
> They're only gonna hurt you,
> In the end!
> Drugs don't mean nothing,
> If you have what it takes!
> So be drug free,
> And you'll be first-rate!

"I know people still think cheerleading is corny and all that," says Pam with a shy voice that belies the raw spirit and energy she demonstrates through her girls. "I know some people make fun of what we do. But all of that is changing. I think we've done a lot for this community, a lot toward bringing everybody together. And I think people appreciate what we've done. Cheerleaders who compete at our level are really world-class athletes. I think people are just starting to recognize that."

Pam's not kidding when she says cheerleaders should be considered world-class athletes. A word of advice from old Willard: Don't offer the age-old show business line for good luck—"break a leg"—to any cheerleader before an important competition. She (or he) may just take you up on it. Pam tells me that one of her girls, a ninth-grader named Shannon, broke her ankle in practice before last year's national championships, but she went on to compete with the team despite her accident. If that's not world-class dedication and team spirit, then I don't know what is.

"The girls really care about cheering," Pam reckons. "They have to, they spend so much time on it. I know when

I left high school, cheering was something I missed, something I wanted to get back to." Pam got back to her first love through her work as a secretary in the principal's office at Hanover School. And—I promise not to tell the principal if you won't!—she considers her duties as cheerleading coach her full-time job.

"I hope some of the girls take my love for cheering away with them when they graduate," Pam admits. "That means a lot to me. But mostly I hope the attitude I've tried to teach sticks with them. There's not much chance to cheerlead out there in the real world, but a good attitude is always important."

When it comes to cheerleading, Pamela Aregood Agnew has got all sorts of the right stuff. She's got the right attitude, and she's full of good cheer.

* *

THE VIEW FROM UP HERE

★ JERRY FOSTER

Cave Creek, Arizona

Jerry Foster is the kind of guy who's up in the air about most things. Actually, pretty much everything about Jerry is up in the air because Jerry spends almost every waking and working moment up in the air—in his helicopter.

As far as I know, Jerry Foster is the only full-time, on-camera television newsman/weatherman who broadcasts his reports from a flying studio. Live. Twice a day. Five days a week. That's how we first met—I was in the Phoenix area on one of my many visits, and Jerry showed me around on behalf of KPNX-TV Channel 12, the NBC affiliate there. And when Jerry Foster shows you around, he really shows you around. We've been great friends ever since, and we get together for a visit whenever we can break away from our busy work schedules.

Jerry's busy work schedule is unlike any I've ever seen or

*I just flip my wig at
what Jerry Foster
sees every day.*

heard tell of. In addition to his news and weathercasting chores for the noon and five o'clock broadcasts, Jerry pulls double duty as an eye in the sky for the Maricopa County Sheriff's Department, doing surveillance and rescue work on a voluntary basis whenever needed. Maricopa, which houses communities in and around Phoenix, is the ninth-largest county in the country, and strange as it may seem, the local sheriff's office is without a chopper. So the sheriff just places a call to good old reliable Jerry whenever he needs a whirly-bird, and Jerry always responds like the true professional he is. He's rescued mountain climbers from a rock slide and saved lost and dehydrated hikers from a barren mountain trail. "A lot of good-intentioned people just go out, and they don't appreciate how rough this country is," Jerry explains. "Every once in a while they need somebody to bail them out."

Of course there are times when common sense escapes the blame in favor of our old friend Mother Nature. One of Jerry's most dramatic rescues occurred during the violent flood of 1984. He received a call at two in the morning alerting him to a father and three-year-old son in distress in a rising river; they had driven their car off the road and were forced from the interior of the car to the hood as the river kept rising. "They were in the middle of the river," Jerry remembers, getting excited all over again in the retelling, "and by the time we got there they were pretty much on tiptoes on the roof of the car. A couple of minutes later and we wouldn't have made it." He catches his breath along with me before continuing. "There's no feeling in the world like saving someone's life. Nothing at all."

His heroic efforts have not gone unnoticed. Several years ago he was honored by President Reagan with the Harmon Trophy, the most prestigious award given to pilots. (Previous winners include Howard Hughes and Charles Lindbergh.) Jerry was singled out for his search and rescue efforts in Maricopa and Pinel counties, and he remembers his visit to the Oval Office to accept the award—alongside the first group of shuttle astronauts—as one of the most exciting moments of his life. "That's a thrill, let me tell you," he says now with a regal grin. A statue honoring award recipients stands proudly in the Air and Space Museum in Washington, D.C.

"I always knew I wanted to fly," Jerry tells me. "Ever since I was a seventh-grader in Duncan, over in the southwest corner of the state. I saw a helicopter flying around outside the school window, and right away that was my dream. I just stared and stared at it through the window, and I knew right then I'd be a helicopter pilot. I guess you could say I had it easier than everybody else, because I knew off the bat what I'd someday be doing."

Of course, he wasn't always doing this for a living. But a local radio station decided it could cut down on costs if the helicopter pilot also handled the traffic reports, so Jerry entered the broadcast business through that back door. "The news stories came later," Jerry says, "partly as a result of all the rescue work that I do. I would keep telling the station managers that it just didn't make sense to have me up there, with all these great pictures, without a camera. Finally, someone listened."

One of the reasons Jerry and his Sky 12 crew have been successful is that they're ready to take off on a moment's notice. Really, he's always at the ready. "We're not here because we're good," he says, "and we're not here because we're smart. We're here because we're prepared. That's an old Boy Scout motto, but it applies to us more than you would think. We can have that chopper up in the air within twenty minutes, any time of day. We're always ready to fly."

But being always ready to take off on one mission or another can sometimes get in the way of other doings. There are no dividing lines with Jerry when it comes to vocation and avocation; his commitment to chopper and community takes a backseat to nothing. Not even his family. "It absolutely does get in the way," Jerry admits with some pain in his voice. "That's what cost me my first marriage. It got to the point where my first wife said to me, 'Jerry, which is more important, me or the helicopter?' That was a tough one. But flying is the love of my life, and I had no choice, not really." (Jerry's second wife of six years shares his passion for flying; they also share a love of scuba diving, and the two of them recover evidence and, sometimes, bodies from local lakes and rivers for the police department.) I can relate, a little bit, to what Jerry went through; it sometimes seems that my career pulls me away from my family too often, and for too long, and I know the push-and-pull he tells me he felt between the people he loved and the work he loved.

Lately, Jerry has developed another hobby that's almost as impressive as his love affair with flying. He raises championship Peruvian Paso horses, a gorgeous Spanish breed of black stallion; his first horse, Rey de Reyes (Spanish for King of Kings), is a big, strong, impressive-looking animal with a muscular neck and a beautiful shiny coat. "If the horse could tell you how good-looking he is, you'd be on the phone with him all day," Jerry jokes.

The business with the Peruvian Pasos came about after Jerry was asked to appear at parades and events as an offshoot of his work with KPNX. "Every time I'd go to one of these things, they'd ask me to ride a horse," he explains. "And every time I was on somebody else's horse, there was trouble. The last thing you want to do is have a grand marshal at your parade who keeps getting thrown by his horse. And then when I got the first one I started thinking, you know, you can't just have one." Jerry now keeps seven prize Peruvian Pasos in his stable, and he is forever trotting out his black beauties to area appearances sponsored by a local con-

venience store chain. He's gosh darn proud of these crea-
tures, and deservedly so.

He lives the good life, my friend Jerry Foster, and he's the
most liberated man I know. I don't mean liberated in any
kind of Alan Alda-Gloria Steinem sense, but liberated from
the constraints that govern most of our lives and life-styles.
Jerry is, literally, free as a bird, to go wherever he wants,
whenever he wants; he's got this wonderful million-dollar
piece of machinery sitting in his backyard forever ready to
take flight, and he's got the beautiful Arizona mountains and
countryside to use as his back streets. He tells me he's found
a doctor and a dentist in the area with landing fields big
enough to accommodate his chopper, and that he's memo-
rized all of the local shopping centers with room enough for
his bird. He even drops his two daughters off at school in the
thing. Can you imagine? "I go everywhere I want to in the
chopper," he says, "any time I want to."

He really does. Once he took me to a wonderful, isolated
little place in the Colorado River canyon—the Little Colorado, he called it—an old Indian reservation where we were
surrounded on all sides by these vast canyon walls, as high
as you could hope to see. The Hopi Indians look on this
magical site as the place where all life began, and I remember looking around and thinking perhaps they knew what
they were talking about. What a fantastic sight! And to think
all of it is pretty much inaccessible to us mere mortals forced
to get around on commercial air carriers or—bite your
tongue!—behind the wheel of an automobile.

A beautiful new world is open to people like Jerry Foster,
a vast new wilderness that is breathtaking to behold. What is
distant and remote and out of the way for most people is as
convenient as a trip to the corner store for Jerry and his family. For my money, Jerry Foster really knows how to live.

★ ★

Two jewels in the museum's Jewel Room—Mary Harris Francis and Barbara Marshall.

IT'S A SMALL WORLD
AFTER ALL

★ **MARY HARRIS FRANCIS & BARBARA MARSHALL**

Kansas City, Missouri

For a couple of big thinkers, Barbara Marshall and Mary Harris Francis really know how to think small.

Together they started Kansas City's acclaimed Toy and Miniature Museum as a place to store and display their collections of all things greatly small. But before they opened their museum doors, you might say their small collections had outgrown themselves. "I was running out of closets," recalls Barbie, an appropriate nickname for a woman who has spent the better part of her adulthood collecting miniature doll furniture. "I quite honestly did not have another inch of space."

In the four years since the museum opened, the collections have grown to somewhat larger proportions, and the two women now boast one of the most precious and prestigious arrays of antique dollhouses, hand-crafted miniatures, and assorted tiny toys you're likely to find this side of Lilliput. Their little treasures are on loving display in a thirteen-room, turn-of-the-century mansion, borrowed from the kind folks at

35

the University of Missouri, Kansas City. It's a perfect setting for a collection that celebrates perfection in miniature. A big kid like me can really lose himself in a place like this, let me tell you.

Friends since childhood, Barbie and Mary Harris, as she is known, did not lock heads on the idea of a museum until they found themselves together in London during one of their many collecting missions. "It's funny," recalls Mary Harris, "we'd known each other all our lives, and it took a trip to England to bring us together on a project like this."

When they returned to the States, they set about launching their project in earnest. "We went straight to the top," says Mary Harris. "We met with the mayor, with the chamber of commerce, anybody we thought could help us. Now, we were known in the community, but I'm what you might call a back-pew sitter, and it was very unlike me to ask people, you know, 'What can you do for us?' We told everybody we wanted to start a museum of antique toys and miniatures, and everybody kept saying, 'You want to do what?' Nobody understood what we wanted to do." But eventually Barbie and Mary Harris found encouragement from the University of Missouri chancellor, and the two were very nearly in business. "Because Kansas City is a small town, the red tape we had to go through was not as red as it could have been someplace else," Mary Harris says.

I'm sure you've got swell folks like Barbie and Mary Harris in your own hometown, folks who share their particular wealth, even when the sharing doesn't come easy. They searched high and low to find the perfect place for their stuff, and when they ran into a brick wall they just turned a corner and kept on going. I admire that.

Barbie and Mary Harris directed an extensive renovation of the university property. "We wanted to make good use of the space," Barbie tells, "but we were careful not to get past the point of intimacy. After all, it would be somewhat of a contradiction to have our collections on display in this huge museum."

And then they moved in.

The museum is now home to more than seventy fully furnished dollhouses, including one, circa 1860, which belonged to the daughter of the man who designed the Tower of London Bridge. It has all the original furnishings, including the hand-stitched carpets thrown by the little girl—Lady Horatia Jones—who was its original proprietor. They've even got a house with stained-glass windows, spiderwebs in the attic, and a tiny cherry pie cooling on the windowsill.

There are some great pieces here. A visitor will also find a room modeled after a Victorian nursery, a working collection of nineteenth-century kitchen objects (originally designed to teach little girls in Nuremberg, Germany, how to work their way around the kitchen), and a colorful depiction of a Chinese wedding procession. The museum also boasts a large collection of frozen Charlotte dolls, which refers to an old-style, rigid, one-piece doll with no moving parts. (Barbie and Mary Harris tell me the name for these dolls comes from a terribly wonderful New England legend, which holds that a mother sent her daughter, Charlotte, out in the cold one evening, with a warning to wear her cape to keep the chill away; daughter Charlotte, as you may have guessed, did not heed her mother's warning, and the frozen Charlotte doll was born. I'm a sucker for a terrible tale like that.)

The detail in everything at the museum is precise, and every piece is in working order, something that matters most of all to Barbie. "The scale has to be correct," she insists, "otherwise I'm not interested. If I have a tea kettle, it pours. If there's a tiny lock on the door, it works. All of my instruments make music. My things cannot be played with. They're delicate and fragile, but you can relate to them. You'd be surprised how many people lose themselves in miniatures. When life gets complicated, we can create our own tiny worlds. It's really quite a wonderful escape."

"My collection is much more clunky than Barbie's," admits Mary Harris. "Scale is not important to me. I want to be able to play with my toys. When my kids were growing up they'd look through these wish-books to see what they wanted for Christmas, and there I'd be, making out my wish-list right along with them. I always spend a lot of time in toy stores, and I can't wait for the kids to go on home so I can belly up to the bar and have some fun."

There are those who might say these two lovely ladies

have lost their grip on reality, that their lifelong passions are little more than the stuff of child's play. Nonsense, I say, and so say the lovely ladies themselves. "I bet if you asked fifty people—I'm talking about grown adults—if they had their original teddy bears, about thirty would say that they did," predicts Mary Harris. Call it a Mary Harris poll, a hunch based on years of holding on to the little girl within her. "I think we all hold on to our fascination for toys a lot longer than people think," she says.

Nevertheless, Barbie and Mary Harris both have to put up with some ribbing over the obscure objects of their desire. Both women are the mothers of grown children, and Mary Harris remembers when visitors would come to call and ask her kids, "Is your kid mother here?" "They'd respond by saying something like 'Mother's busy playing.' Sometimes when I leave for the museum I'll say, 'Well, I'm going to work,' and the whole family will laugh hysterically."

"My three daughters love the fact that I collect," admits Barbie. "They even furnish their own houses now. But when they were younger I wouldn't let them go near my furniture. They couldn't play with Mommy's things."

"It's been a lot of hard work," Mary Harris admits, "but then we look back and realize it's been a tremendous pleasure. Starting a museum like this up from nothing is a challenge, and for two little round ladies we've done all right. We're very proud of ourselves."

"Sure we're proud," adds Barbie. "People are happy when they come in here. On our own small scale, we're able to generate some of the same feeling you get when you step into Disneyland. In our own small way, we do the same thing. There's a certain magical feeling here, it's like another world. You walk through our doors, and right away you know you're someplace special."

Mary Harris even gets philosophical about the museum's growing collection. "Toys reflect reality," she explains. "They leave room for the imagination. And miniatures . . . well, they're really just reality reduced in size."

Small wonders, these two lovely ladies. Stop in if you have the chance.

Bundled up against the cold at the Rockefeller Center Ice Skating Rink with Dr. William P. Foster and the McDonald's All-American High School Band.

FIXIN' TO BEAT THE BAND

★ DR. WILLIAM P. FOSTER

Tallahassee, Florida

Well, we've visited with the queen of America's high school cheerleading coaches, and to continue with our pep rally of school spirit I thought you'd like to meet the man who, more than anybody else, has helped to shape the changing face of another distinctly American institution—the school marching band. He's the best in the business, and his name is Dr. William P. Foster.

When it comes to marching bands, Bill Foster marches to the beat of a different drum majorette. He's done his thing in a big way for Florida A&M University for the past forty-one years, where he serves as director of bands, and in the process he's redefined the way things get done in the marching band business. "Forty years ago, marching bands were really in their infancy," Bill remembers. "Maybe we'd play a song or two, and if we were adventurous, we'd form a letter or two, and that was it. There was nothing like the big themes and production numbers we have today. We've really seen a renaissance."

His first band at Florida A&M, in 1946, was only 45 strong;

today's line-up consists of a heavily recruited 250. "I thought a hundred would be our magic number," says Bill, "but we hit that after only a couple of years, and we've been growing ever since." The band goes by the nickname of "The Marching 100," but the name, Bill says, is really a misnomer. "Somebody called us that early on, and the name just stuck," he says. "We'd be crazy to try and change it."

This man is an artist, and the football fields of America are his canvasses. He has done some incredible things, mixing music and motion to create almost a new art form. The bring-down-the-stadium performances of the Florida A&M Marching Band, under his direction, have been called "the greatest half-time shows in America," and if ever there was truth in advertising, here it is. The Marching 100 has also been called "the Notre Dame of marching bands" (by CBS's "60 Minutes"), "the Lena Horne of marching bands" (by the *Wall Street Journal*), and "the E. F. Hutton of marching bands" (by the *Tallahassee Democrat*). You get the idea.

Every time you see a marching band, at any high school or college from coast to coast, you'll likely see Bill's influence at work. His many innovations include the use of double-time (four steps per beat) and triple-time (six steps per beat) marching steps, the correlation of the instrument arc and the knee lift, and the development of three-dimensional animation in formations. But my favorite innovation is the way he gets tuba and sousaphone players to leap high into the air with their instruments and land in a leg split. Ouch! "Sometimes I wonder myself how these kids can carry those heavy instruments," Bill admits. "This year we've had some pretty tiny people playing some pretty big instruments."

Plain old two-dimensional animation was added to the marching band's repertoire in 1962, and with that now common technique Bill again revolutionized the form. Under his direction, band members formed a football player, with a moving foot to kick the ball. "And the ball wasn't just some ball," Bill explains. "It was a bunch of band members." Similar routines were choreographed for a basketball and a baseball player. "Of course we played 'Sweet Georgia Brown' and 'Take Me Out to the Ball Game' for those two," Bill says. Of course. Until three years ago, the elaborate routines were mapped and plotted on tabletop playing fields, with figurines to represent the band members, but Bill and his full-time staff of four have lately turned to computers for a high-tech assist.

Believe it or not, Bill did his doctoral dissertation on band pageantry—he earned his doctorate of education from Columbia University's Teachers College—and his resulting book, *Band Pageantry,* is widely considered the bible for marching band instruction. "Most themes for half-time shows are based on one of three ideas," Bill asserts. "Events in history, human personalities, and current events." He practices what he preaches, my friend Bill: on the weekend of the first moon walk, The Marching 100 formed a facsimile of the *Apollo* lunar module landing on the moon; another notable "moon walk" several years later (made famous by the light-footed Michael Jackson), was commemorated on the field with a medley of the singer's hit songs and a breakdance routine that looked like something out of a nightclub. "The challenge is being consistently creative and at the same time contemporary," he says.

His most difficult assignment, he says, came during Super Bowl III—in January 1969, when Joe Namath and the Jets shocked our beloved Baltimore Colts—when he was asked to have the band emerge from a jumbo-size horn 'o plenty in the Orange Bowl of Miami. "They wanted us to come out marching and playing," Bill recalls. "That presented all sorts of problems in terms of sound and echo. It took a little work, and some acoustic vision, but we overcame the problems to where we had band members marching out of the horn four abreast, and as they appeared they built to a grand crescendo. It was really quite magnificent."

I've known Bill for the past several years, and our friendship has grown out of his annual visits to the Rockefeller Center skating rink at the helm of McDonald's All-American High School Band. Of course, his charges don't do much in the way of marching at that particular venue ("Oh, no," Bill insists, "not on the ice!"), but they can belt the heck out of any tune. I stand off on the sidelines and watch Bill put his all into what he's done for his entire adult life, and I marvel at his energy, his pure and simple enthusiasm. The music moves him, and it's a pleasure to see. I stand there on the ice and feel warm all over just watching him.

The McDonald's band pulls two high school students from each state and the District of Columbia (and one student each from the Virgin Islands and Puerto Rico). Lately they've been appearing on the "Today" show when the band convenes in New York for the Macy's Thanksgiving Day Parade. The McDonald's band also adds its all-American luster each year to the Fiesta Bowl and Tournament of Roses parades.

Bill has also conducted the United States Air Force Band, the Gamagori Municipal Band of Japan, the National Intercollegiate Band, the United States Army Band, and the Florida A&M University Symphonic Band. He was recently appointed to the Black Music Association Foundation board of trustees. And the FAMU Marching Band was awarded the MVP of marching band awards—the prestigious Sudler Intercollegiate Marching Band Trophy—in October 1986.

Yet for all the awards and honors, Bill doesn't see himself as the biggest innovator the world of marching bands has ever seen. "No, sir," he insists with characteristic humility. "Television has by far been the biggest influence on the band movement. What you see now are almost full-scale television productions, with costumes and narration and a consistent theme. For some of your bigger productions, the show is designed not only for the people in the stadium, but for the people at home. Television changed the way a lot of us planned our performances."

But whether you're watching Bill's wizardry on the small screen or in a football stadium packed to the rafters with screaming fans, you're in for quite a treat. He practices a peculiarly American art form that is also beautiful, spirited, and intense, and practice, in this case, makes perfect.

EVERYWHERE I go, I meet a Jerry Foster or a Pamela Aregood Agnew, someone who has taken a lifelong passion and used it to fuel a community good, people like Mary Harris Francis and Barbara Marshall, whose seemingly trivial pursuits have been affectionately embraced by like-minded neighbors. Or there's a fellow like Bill Foster, a visionary who changes in a big way the way we look at the little things. These are the folks who add texture to my American neighborhood. We're lucky to have 'em.

I remember, growing up, the folks in my actual neighborhood who made the special effort to organize our parades, to stage our community plays, to raise the prize-winning hogs at our local fairs. There were all sorts of dedicated hobbyists back when I was a kid, and they're still out there, lending character to our small towns and big cities. Find the ones in your neck of the woods and say hello for me.

"I thought you said this was a black-tie remote!"—with my working-class colleagues, Jane Pauley and Bryant Gumbel.

3 Working-Class Heroes

"IF a task is once begun, do not leave it 'til it's done," my grandfather used to sing to me. "Be it great or be it small, do it well or not at all."

A pleasant little jingle—it's got a nice, whistle-while-you-work quality to it, don't you think?—and one that can't help ring its way through my head as I think about introducing you to the folks you'll meet in this chapter. A stove repairman, a milkman, and a rent-a-car agent, and all three of them stand for everything that's right and good about our American work ethic; they stand also as proud testimonials on behalf of everyone who works in jobs we tend to take for granted.

You know the people I'm talking about, the folks in our communities who really keep things running easy as a fresh-baked pie—the teachers, the fire fighters, the mail carriers, the clerks at our corner stores.

Throughout my life, I've been lucky enough to rely on kind souls at every turn. I can still remember our old milkman, the way he'd drive around in the heat of summer and treat the neighborhood kids to a block of ice off his truck. If you've never tried it, there's nothing quite like the cooling taste of a hunk of ice that's been resting on the wooden shelves of a milk truck.

I can still remember my Sunday School teachers—Mrs. Draper and Mr. Reno—and I carry around some of what they taught me to this very day. I've still got a vivid picture of Mrs. Draper, a tall, thin woman who always wore a flowered dress bought, probably, for $3.95 at Montgomery Ward. As for Mr. Reno, well, he got his hands on me when I was twelve or thirteen years old, when my values were taking shape, and he's had a lasting influence on me.

Right now, there's a treasure of a man in my life named Colonel Brook, who helps run our Virginia farm for my wife, Mary, and me. To tell you the truth we'd be lost without him. He's not a bona fide colonel or anything, my friend Colonel, that's just his name. He's traced his roots back to the time of George Washington, when his ancestors worked as slaves on our founding father's plantation. Colonel tells me they used to tend to Washington's water system, and they'd purify the water by running it through coals and rocks. That's something you won't pick up in any old history book, but it's the kind of fascinating tidbit Colonel dispenses every day as he goes about his business.

These days the business he goes about is landscaping, and what he does is a damn sight more personal than the services offered by those national lawn care companies you see advertised on the Sunday football games. He puts in the extra effort—like the time he helped me sweat over a gatepost when he'd just stopped by to say hello, or the time he brought us a country sausage cured from a hog he'd killed himself—and he does it with a smile.

That's the key to the whole deal, the smile. And the extra

effort. Skip, the guy who cleans our place, has got it. (And yes, he does do windows.) Bucky Holzinger, our carpenter, has got it. Jay Campbell Kearns, the old-fashioned business-man who sold me my tractor, has got it. Lots of folks have got it, but a lot of them are losing it, I'm afraid. That's why I worry about today's so-called yuppie generation. Sure, they're more aggressive and ambitious than generations be-fore them; sure, they're doggedly determined to succeed. But I can't help thinking something—a little bit—is missing in their hearts. This country has been built on an even bal-ance of givers and takers, but I'm afraid that lately the scales have been tipping toward the side of the greedy.

I don't mean to preach, but I visit with the folks you'll meet in this chapter, and others like them, and I get to wondering what the world would be like if they were the rule and not the exception. It's true, money can corrupt, and the more money a job pays, the less likely a person is to do it for the sheer joy of it. The folks profiled here, you can't pay them enough to do what they do; they're priceless, and their cheer-ful dedication casts them as some of our true national heroes.

★ ★

MR. FIX-IT
★ LEO HOFFMAN
Brooklyn, New York

For a stove and range repairman, Leo Hoffman is some-thing of a celebrity. A few years ago he was called in to do a major repair job on the range of an unsuspecting writer from *The New Yorker* magazine—a fellow who was so taken by Leo's no-nonsense attitude and apparent expertise that he thought to introduce this priceless character to his readers—and ever since this chance and close encounter, Leo's life has taken a turn for the notorious. A major profile in that erstwhile publication led to lesser profiles in less erstwhile publications around the country and, finally, to the ultimate

"I never met a range I couldn't fix."—Leo Hoffman with his wife and granddaughter.

indication of his place in popular culture—an appearance on "Late Night with David Letterman."

Leo handles the limelight so well I figured I'd let him shine in these pages: "I've never met a range I couldn't fix," boasts Leo in his own inimitable fashion, and I'm not about to argue with him on this one. "No, seriously, I mean it, you been doing what I been doing for as long as I been doing it, and, I don't know, I guess you know what you're doing after a while. I know my job." He should; after all, Leo's been fixing ranges for Welbilt, a leading manufacturer of home appliances, going on forty years. I don't know many people who've worked at the same job for so long, let alone for the same company, but Leo's still at it, and he shows no signs of letting up.

"I started out—I'm almost embarrassed to tell you what I was making when I started out," he says, his face deep in the innards of a well-used Welbilt, his hands stretching to the top of the range for a hard-to-reach tool. He grunts and groans with the movement before continuing: "First paycheck was for eighty-nine dollars, if you can believe it. I'm embarrassed to tell you, but that was it, that was it for a whole week."

Watching Leo work, you get the feeling he'd still do what he does for the same $89 a week, except for the fact that he's got a lovely wife and four now-grown kids to worry about. You can't help but look at Leo do his thing and feel like getting down and dirty right alongside him, like rolling up your sleeves and helping out. Put him on a show like "What's My Line," and you wouldn't have all that much trouble figuring out what he does for a living; he looks like a repairman, our friend Leo. He's short and stocky, built low to the ground (the perfect size and shape, really, for a range repairman), with a thinning head of hair and a happy round face under his baseball hat announcing the Welbilt name. "You ask me why I wear a hat," he says before you have a chance to even think about asking. "It's because I've got my head stuck in these ovens all the time, and they're filthy, most of 'em, and I don't want all that stuff rubbing up against the top of my head. It's bad enough I go home smelling like grease and everything without wearing it in my hair, too, if you know what I mean." I think I do, even if I could just take my hair off and let it soak in the sink for a while.

From the looks of things, Leo Hoffman has more fun than you can shake a screwdriver at. He seems to love prancing his way into ten kitchens a day, kibitzing with the folks, troubleshooting the problem, sipping coffee (sometimes he'll call ahead to make sure a cup is ready for him, light with no sugar), announcing the repairman's play by play as he gets down to business, and moving on his merry way. "Sometimes lately people ask me when I'm gonna retire," says Leo, who is sixty, "but what the hell am I gonna retire for? What else am I gonna do? I love this, this is what I do."

I've lived in New York for a few years now, long enough to know that Leo is the typical New Yorker. He's got an opinion on pretty much everything—from city politics to taxicab drivers, teenage drug use to the New York Mets, soup to nuts—and he's not afraid to get a thing off his chest, if he's so inclined. He is forever making long stories short—as in "Let me make a long story short"—except the way he makes them short is by not finishing them, by moving on to something else, to another story similarly abridged. By the end of a repair visit he's likely to leave you cliff hanging with half a dozen unresolved story lines, like the time he fixed the stove of the Israeli ambassador to the United Nations or of actor Darren McGavin. "He's the Night Stalker," Leo says of McGavin. "He's got a nice kitchen." Sometimes you just feel like saying, "Okay, Leo, so what happened in this nice man's nice kitchen?" but by the time you get around to it, Leo's on to something else.

One story he does get around to finishing is his colorful account of his visit to the Letterman show. "My wife, Millie, bought me this beautiful new suit," he remembers, "you know, this Mafia suit, and they sent this Honda stretch limo to pick us up. I had everybody with us, my wife, my kids, my mother-in-law, my little granddaughter. You shoulda seen the back of this thing. I mean, we're talking captain's quarters seats, a bar, a phone, a television. My God, I couldn't believe it. Me, Leo Hoffman. I couldn't get over it, it was really something. I didn't even know Honda made a stretch limo, shows you what I know."

So there they are, Leo Hoffman and family, all dressed up on their way to the Letterman show, and where does he ask the driver to take them? You're gonna love this—to the Off-Track Betting windows in his Bensonhurst neighborhood. "My wife says to me, 'Leo, you're going to OTB? You're crazy!" and I says to her, 'What do I care?' So we pulled around, and I called out all my cronies, Lefty, Zeke, and Tony, and I said, 'Look at me! Can you believe it? Me, Leo Hoffman?!' "

On the trip home after the show, Leo made a few calls on the limousine phone to let friends and family know how things went, to remind them to tune in when the show aired later that night. One of the people he called was his mother. In Florida. "Why not," he says, "what do I care?" One of the wonderful things about a guy like Leo Hoffman, which you can see from this long story made short, is that he's not easily embarrassed; he is comfortable enough with himself to be able to make long-distance phone calls from the backseat of a courtesy limousine. He reminds me a little of yours truly.

But the true stuff of Leo's day to day are almost all kitchen-related, and the thing about fixing stoves in a city like New York is that it gives you a unique perspective on the way most of us live. Leo has seen everything, and he guesses he's paid a service visit to every substantial apartment building in Manhattan. "Most people are pigs," he admits. "Really, they don't know how to clean or take care of their things. I tell 'em, I'm not afraid to tell 'em, if their place is a mess, but' particularly I tell 'em when they haven't been taking care of their range. Most of the problems I get are because people don't clean their range. I've opened up these things, and I've found mice and rats, and grease like you wouldn't believe. They're filthy, people in this city, that's what really gets me. Some of these things look like they haven't been cleaned since they were installed, and they call me in and wonder why the thing is broken. Sometimes they just don't know how to use the thing, and they wonder why it's broken. It's broken because you broke it, dummy, because you didn't take care of it. I didn't break it, Welbilt didn't break it, you broke it." He tells his filthy customers to turn over a new leaf, but to stay away from most oven-cleaner products. "That stuff's for Tony Randall, not for you," he says. Instead, he advises people to use soapy water and ammonia for cleaning, and to use basic WD-40 oil to lubricate the door hinges.

"I'm like a doctor," Leo says, the voice of philosophy and reason. "Really, you call me in, there's a problem, you know, a crisis, something's wrong, and it needs fixing. People wait for me to come in, just like a doctor, and fix the problem. It's not something they can do for themselves, they need a professional. I'm a professional, and if I can't fix it, then they've got to go eat at Wendy's."

And that, to make a long story short, is the end of that.

* *

SHE TRIES HARDER, YOU BETTER BELIEVE IT

★ ELIZABETH KIDWELL

Birmingham, Alabama

If you're like most people, you've probably never given a rent-a-car agent a second thought, but if you're like most people, you haven't rented a car from Elizabeth Kidwell. Liz has been checking folks in and checking folks out for Avis

Rent-a-Car for nearly twenty-three years, and she says that's the hardest part of her job, being taken for granted. I always try to be especially nice to people who work in jobs like Liz's, but ever since I met Liz I've been making an extra-special effort.

"I have often said that people look at certain types of people and say, 'You are part of the woodwork,' " she explains with a deep southern accent that doesn't stand out quite so much in her part of the country as it might someplace else. "You know how they look right at you and still it seems like they're looking someplace else? I work in one of those jobs where people think I'm one of those types of people, and one of these days I'm gonna grab somebody by the collar and holler, 'Hey! Pay attention to me! Please!' Sometimes I just wanna yell here, there, and yonder to someone who's not listening, someone looking right through you."

But she doesn't yell, this magnificent lady. Instead she just smiles and chalks it up to human nature. Actually, she chalks up a lot of what she sees to human nature. "Really, it's so humorous dealing with the public," she says. "You can try your best and give someone really thorough directions, real exact, and what kills you is the fool looks at you and says, 'What did you say?' And you wanna laugh and say, 'Sorry, you missed it,' but you can't. Sometimes you have to try really hard."

And even though she works for a company whose motto is "We Try Harder," Liz Kidwell tries harder than most. She bakes cakes and cookies for her regular customers. She'll handle a businessman's dry cleaning while he's in town on appointments. She'll race home to her own liquor cabinet on a Sunday night when the bars and liquor stores are closed, and she'll mix drinks for her customers with a long wait between flights. She'll claim and hold a customer's luggage if he's running late, and if the luggage has been rerouted, she'll help track it down. (God, what I wouldn't give to have a Liz Kidwell to help find some of my lost bags!) And if the customer himself has been rerouted and finds himself stuck in Birmingham with no hotel reservations, well, he can stay at Liz's place. Really. And these are just some of the things Liz Kidwell does for a living.

"I'm a firm believer in making an extra effort in everything I do," Liz says. "It's a personal thing for me. I don't do it for my company, Avis, and I don't do it for my customer's company. I do it for the customer. It's between me and him. Sure, Avis benefits, and the other company benefits, but that doesn't matter. I just keep it one to one, me and the customer. They're like family, my customers, I get so involved in their lives, I see 'em so often, some of 'em I think the world of. I'm close to a lot of 'em. I even dream about some of 'em. My customers are special to me, and there's nothing they can ask me to do that would be too outlandish. There isn't anything I haven't been asked. The only thing that's never been up for grabs is me." She laughs.

When she started in this thing, Liz had no idea what she was getting herself into. "Back then the minimum wage was $1.25 an hour," she says, "and when I came to work that's about what I made. It's not exactly the best-paying job in the world, but it was a job and the hours were good and so I took it." Now, though, the job has become a substantial part of her life, and though she jokes about leaving someday, I get the feeling she never will. Over the years she's worked other jobs, trying to make ends meet as the single mother of three kids, but this job has been the one constant in her working life. A lot of us wear our jobs on our hearts, I know I do, but Liz lives and breathes it more than most people I know.

"Look," she explains, "it's not exactly a job where they appreciate someone with experience. To tell you the truth, from the looks of some of the girls they hire here, you'd think the only thing you need to be is cute. They'll put up with a lot for cute, but the customers know where to go if they want to get treated right. My hair is gray and I'm forty-nine years old, but I've got a lot more to offer than looks. People with a problem line up behind the lady with the gray hair. They know I'll take care of them."

By now, Liz has moved up the ranks to where she's earning top pay of $7.60 an hour, but she takes home more than her paycheck each week. She takes home the warm and priceless feeling of a job well done, and she takes home a network of deeply devoted new friends from every corner of this great country. She gets more Christmas cards than she has room to display, and she's been getting birthday cards from one loyal customer for over twenty years.

Liz tells this great story about one of her regular customers, a "sweet little guy" who worked as an executive with Rockwell, which is headquartered in her area. "He would come in, every three or four months, and he'd always have a joke or a trick, something. The man was a scream," she says. "Of course he was comin' in early, early in the morning, there was no one else in the airport but us, so he had to do something to amuse himself."

One morning, the sweet little guy sought to amuse himself and Liz with a puzzle—a huge screw he defied her to unscrew. "You know, it was one of those bigger-than-usual jobs, and he challenged me to undo the nut from the bolt," Liz says. "Well, I tried every way under the sun. I twisted and pulled and pushed 'til I was blue in the face, but nothing doing." Of course, Liz's blue tint turned to red when her Rockwell customer completed his own trick with a simple flick of the wrist, and that, Liz thought, was that.

But here's where the story gets good. Turns out the guy disappeared for a year or so, long enough so Liz got to wondering what happened to him. She keeps tabs on her regular customers, and when one strays from routine she gets worried. She was used to seeing Mr. Laughs every three or four months, and when she hadn't seen him for over a year, she began to think he'd been reassigned. Then, during one busy afternoon (they were three deep at the checkout counter), Liz hears a holler from the balcony overlooking her station. "It was him," she recalls. "I never forget a face, and he's yelling out to me, 'Hey! I bet you don't remember me!' and I yelled right back up to him, 'Sure I do! You're the man with the unusual screw!'

"A hush fell over the terminal, and everybody started laughing and looking at me," Liz says now, still slightly embarrassed at the misunderstanding. "Everybody was staring at me, and I said, 'Well, he is,' and that just got everybody laughing and starting up all over again. I couldn't do a stinking thing about it. Boy, I wish I had a nickel for every time I've put my foot in my mouth."

Liz Kidwell wishes she had a nickel for a lot of things she's done. Like for every kid she's helped get home for the holidays, even when the kid was underage and underqualified for standard company rental policy. Or for every time she's sewn up a businessman's pants while her charge awaited bashfully in the little businessman's room. But, like I said, her payment comes in other forms. "It's nice when someone passes my name on to another customer," she says. "All the time, people come up to me saying, 'So-and-so said to rent a car from you and only from you.' That's nice. What it all comes down to is the people, that's the best part of this job. You see so many things in a job like this, so many people. The world passes before you. I'm not anybody special, I'm just ordinary people, ordinary overworked, underpaid people. But when my customers come up to the counter and all, it's like family coming home. I can't think of anything else I'd rather be doing."

And when she's had a rough day, when too many people look through her as though she's part of the woodwork, when she's just had it up to here with the way some people can be, this wonderful gray-haired lady who's done more for her company than a fleet of new cars just shrugs it off. "Tomorrow's another day," she says, echoing another famous character from the South, "and I never know what will happen. I'm anxious to see if anybody can pull anything new on me."

Me too.

* *

"I ALWAYS THOUGHT JUNIOR LOOKED LIKE THE MILKMAN"

★ BOB HARDY, SR.

Menomonee Falls, Wisconsin

The milkman cometh. Actually, the milkman goeth. Home delivery in the dairy business is almost a thing of the past, but around the country you can still find an occasional holdout, a few strong, cold-smelling men who bring fresh milk

*Milkman Bob Hardy, Sr.,
flanked by his two sons.*

and cheese and eggs to some lucky folks each morning. I remember our milkman from when I was a kid, just like it was yesterday. I mentioned earlier about how he let us have at the blocks of ice off his truck at the end of a hot summer day, but he was always doing a little extra something for the neighborhood kids. Sometimes he'd let us ride with him in the truck, help him out on his run, or sometimes he'd stop in just to shoot the breeze, ask how we were doing in school, things like that.

They're a dying breed, milkmen, what with the skyrocketing costs of gasoline and glass bottles and the like, but they still exist in some parts of the country. I wish they still existed in mine. Gosh, how I loved to take an icy swig of milk, straight from the bottle! I miss that.

The corner store has replaced the milkman in the big cities, the twenty-four-hour supermarket offers his services in our rural communities. The cost-effective way we work and live has curdled the nature of the dairy industry, and the milkmen who were put out of commission by societal and economic changes were driven to other areas of the dairy business. Our life and life-styles may have changed in the process, but theirs hasn't gone sour as a result. They still get up before the sun to deliver the stuff fresh each morning.

Bob Hardy delivered milk on home delivery routes for nearly eleven years, for the Golden Guernsey Dairy, the largest dairy in the Milwaukee area, before turning to wholesale deliveries to make a living. "I could see the handwriting on the wall," he remembers of his decision to buy his own wholesale delivery route from the dairy in 1970. "I could see home delivery going down, slowing down. The dairy was losing routes."

Being a milkman was tops for Bob as a young man, what he always wanted. He joined the dairy in 1958 as a mechanic earning $5,200 a year, but always he had his sights set on a home delivery route. "To me that was excitement, that was adventure. Every day I'd go to the sales manager and pester him," Bob recalls. "There I was, every day, going, 'Any routes open? Any routes open?' and finally there was." His first assignment, for which his salary was upped to $6,000, was an apartment route, the runt of the available route litter, but a route nonetheless. "The fellas hated apartment routes," he says. "You'd have to go up and down, up and down the stairs all the time. You'd load those little wire baskets with as much as you could carry, and then you'd have to come back down for more." But because he was low man in the pecking order of things, he took what he could get. "I was young," he says, "and I was aggressive, and I figured I'd just give it my best."

His best was more than good enough, and it wasn't long before he was out delivering to one of Milwaukee's nicer suburban communities. By then his lot was much better, but it was still a tough way to make a buck. It's a hard life, the life of a milkman. When he was on the home delivery routes, Bob would get to work at about four-thirty in the morning, when he would load his own truck with the heavy wooden milk crates and glass bottles common to the period. "People don't realize, but a lot of sweat goes into the loading," Bob explains. Of course, prior to the loading he'd have to go to the ice house and ice up the racks and the small icebox that would hold excess milk overnight. In those days he'd be driving one of those old stand-up, snub-nosed milk trucks, and the entire bed and storage area was cooled by ice. (Mod-

ern technology, unfortunately, has done away with that pro-
cedure.) Usually he'd finish his route by noon.

Eventually he was made the dairy's "rider foreman" at a
top salary of $14,000 a year, and it was at that level, after
eleven years in home delivery, that Bob decided to get out.
"The dairy was selling off wholesale routes, and I thought
that was the future for me," he says now, looking back. "All
the guys I worked with, they told me I was crazy. I was going
off salary, going off benefits, vacations, going to work for
myself, and they thought I was nuts. But I knew we were
losing home delivery routes pretty fast, and I knew pretty
soon I wouldn't have a job." He paid the dairy $1,100 for his
route, which entitled him to all wholesale deliveries in his
area, and he paid $2,000 for his first truck—a sixteen-foot
electronically refrigerated baby he'd have to plug in every
night to allow enough time for the ice banks to form on the
walls and ceiling. He's been on his own, and making a good
living, ever since. (His foresight was twenty-twenty: Golden
Guernsey no longer employs home delivery men; the few
routes remaining are individually owned by enterprising
milkmen like Bob Hardy.)

Now that he works for himself (one of his two sons works
with him), Bob puts in longer hours than ever before. Sometimes he's on the job fifteen, sixteen hours, six days a week,
delivering to schools, restaurants, mom and pop stores, ho-
tels, and supermarkets. "I still do all the small stops myself,"
he says, "and I let my son handle the bigger deliveries. I'm
thrilled to have him. If I didn't, I'd have to hire two people
to do the work he does."

But even though business, on his own, has been good to
him, Bob sometimes misses his home delivery days. "They
talk about how the baby looks like the milkman, you know
all the jokes, but I never heard any of that on my route," he
says with a smile. Once, though, he opened a server door to
a kitchen, the kind where there's a door inside a door for
deliveries, and he got the surprise of his milk-delivering life.
"The kitchen door was wide open," he recalls, "and there
was this pretty girl sitting at the table, stitch-stark naked,
reading a newspaper. Didn't have a thing on, and she hardly

looks up from her newspaper and she says, 'Good morning, milkman.' That's the way it was a lot of the time—you're accepted as part of the family, part of the day. People tend to be very nonchalant around you, almost like they'd take you for granted or something. I'd just knock on the door and say, 'Milkman!' and go right on in, and people, they'd just be going about their business." Sometimes he'd stop for a cup of coffee or for a chat, but usually he was too worried about finishing his route before all the ice in his truck melted away and the merchandise went bad on him.

One of Bob's favorite stories is about something that happened to a colleague of his—darn the luck!—who filled in for Bob one morning on a delivery to a girls' dormitory at Marquette University. "He was coming down the hall," Bob tells, "when this gal comes out of the shower room without a stitch of clothing on. She says to him, 'I guess it would be foolish of me to run now,' and he says, 'Yes, I guess it would,' and she just walks away back to her room. You hear stories like that once in a while."

Despite some medical reports to the contrary, Bob is a champion of the dairy products that have kept him in business all these years. "Milk is still the best food value around," he insists. "It's the cheapest food you can buy, when you think about everything it gives you. And it's the most perfect drink there is." He drinks more than his share, but his wife doesn't touch the stuff. "She's never liked it," he admits.

"Time goes so fast when I'm delivering," Bob says. "I know I put in long hours, and I'm always working, but I'm always racing the clock, always fighting time. Sure I get up early, and now I get up earlier than when I was on home delivery, but then I look up at the clock and the day's almost gone. It's hard work, but the time goes, let me tell you."

EVERY once in a while I have a lousy day. I guess we all do, but I sometimes feel mine are lousier than most. Anyway, I had a doozy of a lousy day not too long ago, I was all the way down in the dumps, and I was just shuffling around town where I live, trying to shake the doldrums. Well, I wandered into a corner drugstore, a place where Mary and I get a lot of our medication and sundry items, and I slumped down against the counter and asked for a cup of coffee. I wasn't shopping, didn't need anything, just figured I'd as soon pass the next few minutes there as anywhere else. Who knows, maybe I thought a cup of coffee would give me the quick pick-me-up I needed.

So there I was, spreading gloom and doom about the place, when the delightful woman behind the counter turned and said to me, "Willard! What's got you?"

You know, I had no idea, and I told her so.

"Then what are you so down about?" she wanted to know, and before I had a chance to answer she was onto another subject, trading local gossip and chitchat and this and that and the other thing. I'll tell you this, she took my mind off my troubles, whatever they were. And on top of all this, she didn't even charge me for the cup of coffee. "This one's on me," she said.

She gave me a boost when I needed it most, the kind of boost people like Leo Hoffman, Liz Kidwell, and Bob Hardy are handing out all the time. I don't know where we'd all be without folks like them, folks who care about what they do and about the people they serve, who go the extra mile without being asked. Let's hope we never have to find out.

Me and Sally and Mary and Mary.

4 For Better, For Worse

MY father did the dishes. He also did the laundry, and the floors, and pretty much whatever he could to help out. Looking back, it seems he did about as much as my mother to keep our household shipshape.

It's funny how a husband like that would today be considered liberated. Liberated from what? I didn't know any different as a kid, and I don't know any different now.

Actually, I did know different then, come to think of it. My grandparents on my mother's side divided up their household chores over what we might consider a more traditional line. They had a busy, active farm when I was a kid, and my grandmother would spend the entire day—literally—in the kitchen, first with breakfast, then with lunch (or, correctly, dinner, because it was the big meal of the day), and then with supper in the evening. She'd serve up feasts for a dozen or so hungry hands, and in between spreads she'd be busy with the canning, and cleaning, and the general whatnot. She worked as long and hard at what she did as my grandfather did at his chores, but the roles were somewhat more conventional than they were with my mom and dad.

They were quite a pair, my folks. My father could cuss and kick up some dust with the best of 'em, but he was good people, as they say in that part of the country. Underneath his sometimes ornery temper beat a heart of gold. My mother . . . well, she was a jewel. Really, I got as much from her on the importance of family and commitment as I did from anybody. They took care of each other, and me, but they did it their own way. I've never seen a marriage, from the inside or out, work quite the way theirs did.

My marriage is anything but conventional. I'm on the road so much that Mary and I find ourselves curling up with a warm pillow more often than we curl up with each other. Even when I'm not traveling, I spend the work week in New York City, while Mary's either at our home in Virginia or off doing some traveling of her own. A setup like that might seem a recipe for divorce, but Mary and me, we've held up just fine. It's nothing like either of us expected when we tied the knot (to tell the truth, we didn't know what to expect), but we've weathered the changes in our life-style because we fit each other like a comfortable pair of socks: she's independent, I'm independent; she does her own thing, I do mine. She's got her group of friends, I've got mine. I run around the country, hustling up a living, and Mary runs our social life. We may eat out more often than we eat in, and we may eat apart more often than we dine together, but we fill each other's bill of fare. Yes, sir.

But even if we lived a more traditional life-style—nine to five, dinner at six, news at eleven—a marriage like ours wouldn't work if it weren't for our deep, abiding respect for each other. I know, I know, talk is cheap, and it's all too easy to lay a claim to that kind of respect, but with Mary and me it's true as can be. We've built something that can outlast even a crazy schedule like ours, and it's something we're both proud of, believe me. There's a solid foundation there, and that's why it's worked.

And just as our marriage—all twenty-eight years' worth—is a reflection of the marriages of our parents and our grandparents, our children's relationships have and will be influenced by our own. I think about it, and I figure all of this had to rub off on our two daughters. Monkey see, monkey do. Our Mary (or little Mary, to help you keep things straight) and her husband, Don, have got something like the same thing going for them; they run a Domino's Pizza franchise together out in California, and they're a perfect fit. And Sally, our youngest, well, she's a few years away from marriage, but when she gets there you can bet she'll call on some of what she's seen with us to help make it work. In our family Sally's always been the peacemaker, and a role like that grows out of its own kind of respect for others.

I'm a sucker for a happy marriage, mine or someone else's. Pop surveys tell us that more people want to get married today than ever before. *USA Today,* the paper of record as far as I'm concerned, reported in January that 72 percent of single women and 60 percent of single men wanted to get married in 1987. I guess people are tired of hopping from one bed to another, of relationships that just don't go anywhere. Of course, the fear of AIDS and certain social diseases could have a legitimate effect on a poll like that, but people seem to want to put down roots, to find someone to commit themselves to, to start a family, and I'm all for it.

It's funny that in my short life I've lived through the Depression, women's liberation, and the sexual revolution, and here we are once again celebrating the traditional values of marriage and family. We're getting back to basics, and I'm glad all over about it. I don't want to bore you with religion, but indulge me for just a second. The Bible is a book of laws, and the rules and principles you'll find within it are not meant to punish those who stray, but to serve as guidelines for those of us who want some direction. Sure, sex is one of the most pleasant ways to pass the time that I can think of, but face it, it's just not something we can enjoy anytime, anywhere, with anyone we choose. (Darn!)

Look, we all have our weaknesses (even a religious family man like Jimmy Carter has lusted a time or two in his heart), but a good marriage can survive pretty much anything if it's built on a rock-solid foundation of love, respect, and honesty. We've built on that foundation in our home, and I think you'll find the same prime materials went into the marriages you'll read about here.

★ ★

Dawn and David Campbell on their wedding day, with an uninvited guest.

THE NEWLYWED GAME

★ DAWN & DAVID CAMPBELL
Dallas, Texas

I bet you didn't know that Laredo, Texas, boasts the lowest divorce rate in the country. Really, it's true. You'll find less divorces there per thousand marriages than you will in any other city in the country, and the locals are hard-pressed for an explanation. Some say it has something to do with the water or the climate, and others say it has more than a thing or two to do with the deep religious roots in the community, the loyal work ethic that pervades the area. But some, in fact most, just can't figure it at all.

A bunch of us working on a television pilot for Columbia Pictures Television thought it might be fun to get to the bottom of the bottom line in divorce rates, so we packed up our troubles and traveled down to the streets of Laredo to check things out. The crew had their cameras in tow, and we worked our way around town looking for answers. We talked to married couples in all shapes and sizes, folks who've been hitched to the same bedpost for going on fifty years. Fifty years! And try as they might, the good people of Laredo still couldn't put their fingers on why marriages there last longer and stronger than anywhere else.

We were about ready to abandon our search when we thought to look in on a newly married couple, to see if there might be something in the exchanging of vows that would give us some answers, to see if maybe by looking at things from the fresh perspective of the altar, we might be able to get a handle on the situation. On the day we were in town, there were more than a few marriages taking place, as you might expect, but the local chamber of commerce pointed us in the direction of Dawn and David Campbell—in part, David now figures, "because we made a cute couple."

He's right about that, they do make a cute couple, but most of the credit for that goes to David's lovely bride, Dawn (nothing personal, David, but she does have a notch or two on you in the looks department). These two sweet kids were kind and gracious and free-spirited enough to allow a bunch of Hollywood-type strangers to attend and film one of their most personal moments (I'm talking about the ceremony, not the honeymoon—ba-dump-bump), and I'll be forever grateful for their open-hearted hospitality.

I don't know if you've ever attended a wedding where you knew not a soul, but it is quite something. Try it, if you ever have the chance. You really listen to the vows in that kind of situation, and you get to thinking about what the whole institution of marriage means, what it stands for. There I was, sitting in a pretty little church in Laredo, Texas, far away from hearth and home and watching a pretty young couple pledge their lives to each other as a few hundred of their close friends and family members looked on. I was a third wheel—I think all of us in the crew felt we were encroaching on something bigger than a television show, something bigger certainly than a television pilot that would likely never see the light of day—but the ceremony really hit home for me. I'm a sucker for a good wedding.

They're quite a couple, these two kids. Actually, the story

of their courtship fits in neatly with the times, something right off the personals page. They met in a health club, of all places, and Dawn gets the credit for making the first move. (Gosh, I love the way times have changed from when I was a single fella.) "We were both living in Austin," David recalls, "and I'd be pumping my weights and Dawn would be doing her aerobics, and once in a while she'd come into the weight room to do some lifting. I used to notice her and her sister come in, and it was like love at first sight."

But David is on the shy side, and, love at first sight notwithstanding, he didn't say anything, not even hello. "I was beginning to think, you know, he's really stuck-up," Dawn says, smiling. "We pass each other in the gym something like five thousand times a night, everybody says hello to everybody else, and he's not saying anything. Finally I decided I'd say hello to him and see what happened."

They're both glad she did. Hello led to dinner the next night, and the night after that, and the night after that, and the rest has been quite a history. "I don't think we've missed a night since then," David guesses, "at least not when we were in the same town."

Theirs was a whirlwind romance, at least by today's standards: they met in September of 1985, became engaged five months later, and were married in the summer of 1986, all of it less than ten months after they met and merged their health club memberships into a lifetime two-for-one deal.

"I don't think either one of us was thinking about getting married before we met each other," admits Dawn, who is twenty-five. "It wasn't like we were thinking, Okay, it's time for me to find someone and get married. It wasn't like that at all. David was what got me thinking about marriage."

Of course, marriage is not without its adjustment periods. "The first thing I did was take David's car pictures off the wall and put up my pretty paintings," Dawn says, laughing. I listen to these two, just starting out, and I can't help but think back to some of the adjustments Mary and I made during our first days as husband and wife. I'm not an easy guy to live with, I'll be the first to tell ya, but there were things about Mary, too, that took some getting used to. She liked her eggs one way, I liked mine another; she liked a certain side of the bed, and so did I. But those were the simple things. The biggest adjustment we had to make was getting used to the fact that there would always be this other person underfoot. It was tough, but those were some wonderful times. I'm young at heart, reliving those days through Dawn and David.

"Of course, we had to learn to make two of everything," Dawn jokes. "But seriously, you do have to think about turning to someone else for every major decision you make. Every major decision is a group decision. We always have to call each other to see what we think." The first major decision, of course, was where to live, and the couple settled on Dallas, where David, also twenty-five, works in his family's foreign-car salvage business and Dawn works as an interior designer.

"It gets better every day," David says of his marriage. "It's beautiful and wonderful and romantic and all that kind of stuff, but it's also hard work. You do have to work at it, just like you have to work at any relationship, but it's worth it." And is he worried at all that, even with a send-off in a marriage-friendly community like Laredo, the statistics on the long-term success of new marriages leave oddsmakers with a toss-up, at best? "Not at all," he says. "Statistics and divorce and all that, that's for people with hang-ups. Relationships don't work when other things get in the way, when people have too much going on. But when you love each other and that's all there is, then a relationship will always work. If it's important, you'll make it work."

Perhaps that says it all, when it comes to making a marriage work. Statistics, in the long run, don't mean any old thing. It's nice that Dawn and David's marriage got a head start in a divorce-free place like Laredo, Texas, but setting alone is not going to keep these kids married into their golden years. For that they've got to look into their hearts, and from what I've seen of the view, they're sure to find big portions of the right stuff when they go looking.

"And besides," Dawn tells me, "I never knew about Laredo and its low divorce rate until you came to town. God, the situation in the rest of the world must really be bad, because to me Laredo's always been like a soap opera."

So there you have it. I can't wait for the next episode of "As Laredo Turns."

★ ★

You need a wide-angle lens to keep the Veldman family in focus.

"FIFTEEN KIDS! IMAGINE THAT!"

★ **BERNARD & FLORENCE VELDMAN**
Mishawaka, Indiana

If it's true that with six you get egg roll, well, then with fifteen you should be entitled to the whole darn restaurant and all the tea in China.

Bernard and Florence Veldman are the proud parents of, at last count, fifteen children. That's right, fifteen. And they've been married only twenty-six years. Of course, not all the children were born into this big, loving family; a good many have been absorbed into it over the years. Only five of the Veldmans' children are "homemade," as Florence likes to call them; the rest are imported. Seven are adopted (including two Vietnamese sons, two Korean daughters, two American sons, and an American daughter), and three are foster children. Together, they range in age from six to twenty-three. A few from this wellspring of offspring are off at college, but most are still living at home.

I had the pleasure of meeting the whole lot of them at the White House, when they were honored in the American Family Society's Great American Family Awards program, which is chaired by Nancy Reagan. I've been emceeing the awards ceremonies since the program began in 1983, and I've never been so taken with the ties that bind a family, particularly such a large family, as I was when I met the Veldmans. When we were introduced I couldn't shake thinking about that old nursery rhyme, the one about the little old lady who lived in a shoe (she had so many children she didn't know what to do); I imagined kids just busting all over the place, and my heart went out to them, both in sympathy and in admiration.

We did a segment on the "Today" show on the morning of the ceremonies, and I'm told they warmed the big hearts of big families across the country with their extraordinary story. I'm not surprised, because when you meet Bernard and Florence Veldman, the first thing you notice is their overflowing generosity, their full-fledged celebration of a uniquely American spirit of family. The trip to Washington, they tell me, was special not only for the honor, but for the chance to take the whole family on a vacation. "They'd never been on a plane before," Florence says of her kids, "or in a hotel. That was the most thrilling part of the whole thing."

Air travel and hotel accommodations are some of the small luxuries you have to give up when you decide to have children in bunches, but that's all right with the Veldmans. "We always wanted a big family," Florence explains. "Even when we were dating, before we decided to get married, we'd talk about how we wanted to have twelve children." (I don't know about you, but I can think of a few other things to talk about on a first date.)

"I just loved kids," Bernard says. "We both wanted a lot of kids."

Well, then it's a good thing these two caring, lovely people bumped into each other. They met at church (Bernard's brother introduced them), and right away it was a match made in heaven. "I knew as soon as I went out with him he was the guy I wanted," Florence recalls. "You know how sometimes you just know something is right? Well, I just knew it."

Their courtship was a simple one. "We used to go to places that didn't cost a lot of money," Bernard says, "or sometimes places that didn't cost any money. I was a poor college student, and we wanted to save money for our future life together, so we went on hikes and walks and talks. It's true what they say about the best things in life being free. We really got to know each other right away, we talked about important things."

I can't say enough about these two good people. They've opened their hearts and their home to abused and unfortunate children in their area, even though it hasn't always been easy. It sometimes seems there aren't enough hours in the day to meet the time demands of raising such a large family, and the pocketbook doesn't always go as far as it should in meeting those other demands. The family lives on Bernard's earnings as a self-employed mechanical engineer, and Florence helps make ends meet with her talents as a smart shopper. "She knows how to make the dollar go a long way," Bernard boasts. "We can a lot, we freeze a lot, and we stock up on any items that might be on sale or something."

Florence is not only a smart shopper; she's also shrewd. "If they have a limit at the store on a sale item, you know, like one per customer, I'll give one to each child," she lets on. "There's more than one way to skin a cat." I suppose there is.

When they reach the age of sixteen, the Veldmans let their kids take part-time jobs, if they so choose. The only restrictions they place on their children is that they can't work during the week. Weekends are fine, everything else is out. "That makes it tough for them to find jobs, but eventually they do if they look hard enough," Florence says. "You'll always find someone who appreciates a kid who's dedicated to his schoolwork." Bernard and Florence don't ask that their kids contribute to the family coffers, but sometimes, in a pinch, they do. All the children, even the little ones, pitch in around the house with assorted chores.

Their house in Mishawaka, Indiana, on the outskirts of

South Bend, is modest for a family of such overwhelming proportions. It's the same house they moved into when they had but four children of their own, and now, even with their expanding population, they've still only got five bedrooms to work with. There's a big, country-style kitchen (and three full-size freezers, for the overstock), a large, dormitory-style bedroom that sleeps several, and an all-purpose family room. If you can believe it, there's only one full bath, although the two half-baths come in handy at bedtime and when the household is aflutter each morning before school. "In a house like this, with all these people, you don't get much privacy," Bernard admits. Well, I must admit, that comes as no surprise to this intrepid reporter.

With such a bustling and bursting-at-the-seams household, Bernard and Florence don't get much time to themselves, let alone with each other. "We very much cherish our time together," says Florence. "We have some really neat friends, and once in a while they'll go away and offer us their house to use as a kind of retreat. Even if it's for just one or two nights, it's something special."

But even when it's business as usual at the old homestead, it's something special. They really take a devoted interest in each and every one of their children, homemade and otherwise, and they try to spend some special time and caring with one and all. Every night, before bed, Florence and Bernard discuss each child at length and try to determine if anyone is in need of special love and attention. "We try to know where they are all the time," Florence says, and she seems to mean this in an emotional as well as physical sense. Over the years it's developed that each of the older children takes a younger kid under his or her charge to help with the details of caring that might otherwise get lost in the big family shuffle—they read each other bedtime stories, help with homework, braid each other's hair, play ball, that sort of thing.

Everybody pulls together to help make this family work. "People sometimes ask us if our natural-born children feel neglected," Florence says, "but it's not that way at all. They were the ones who first pushed us to take in some of the other kids. One time they went on strike for two weeks to convince us to adopt a child. We're really blessed with the best children in the world, all of our children."

One of the many things that has helped keep this family together is Bernard and Florence's decision, in 1980, to turn off the family television. I know my new bosses at General Electric and the old guard at NBC are not exactly thrilled to hear me say it, but it's true. "They were just watching too much television," Florence explains of her children's behavior before the video blackout. "They'd just be watching it for the sake of watching it, so we decided that during the week there'd be no television. Period. Ever since, their grades have picked up, and they've developed other interests. They weren't too happy about it at first, but they've found other things to keep them busy. Now they talk to each other and play with each other and do things together."

(Take heart, GE and NBC, there is one exception to the house rules: the entire family gathers around the television set on Thursday evenings to watch "The Cosby Show," a program that champions many of the values of sharing and caring fostered in the Veldman household. I'm sure that when the Nielsen folks get wind of the fact that all these Veldmans are watching NBC on only one television set, they'll adjust their national ratings accordingly.)

"Not everyone was meant to have this many children," Bernard says, and he's right about that. But the Veldmans, believe it or not, are now and again meant to have more. At one particularly hectic time, they had eighteen children living under their one small roof. Over the years they've taken forty foster children under their protective and nurturing wings, for stays ranging from several weeks to several years. "If you call us a week from now, we might have a few extra ones," Bernard jokes.

All this love and caring can't help but rub off on Bernard and Florence's relationship. "Oh, we're more in love with each other now than we were twenty-five years ago when we got married," Bernard figures.

"We've given each other the greatest gift you could possibly give," Florence says. "A family."

Boy, have they ever.

★ ★ ★

I ALWAYS tell people that the reason Mary and I have been together for so long is that we hardly see each other. It's become sort of a standard laugh line for me over the years, but it is just that—a laugh line. The truth of it is we see each other plenty, every chance we get, and it tears us apart to be separated as often as we are.

Of course, when we first got married, I stayed in one place. I worked long, hard hours, sure, but I was always able to come home at night. We had no way to anticipate the topsy-turvy, all-over-the-place schedule that would come later with the "Today" show; it's not exactly the kind of thing you can plan for, the way we live today, so we didn't. We were prepared for it, though, because of the things that went into our marriage in the first place. When the chance came for me to appear on a national news program, and everything that went with it, we jumped at it. Imagine, little Willard Scott on grand old NBC, from coast to coast! It was too good to pass up, we both agreed. We didn't know how it would work out, Mary and I, but we decided we'd always regret it if we let the chance pass us by. Plus, we knew we'd always have each other, and we were smart enough to know we'd never lose sight of that.

Who knows how long this wonderful ride will last? But I do know that when it's over, and it will end someday, we'll go back to the way we were. (Gosh, it sounds like I'm talking about Streisand and Redford here, doesn't it?) For now—I'm tapping against my skin head here—knock wood; things are working out just fine.

The impossible dream . . .

5 Against All Odds

I ALWAYS bet on the underdog, and when I've got no money on the line I just root like crazy.

Probably that's because I've always been something of an underdog myself. Just look at me. Flip to any picture of me in this book, and what do you see? You see a celebrity diet book waiting to happen. Right? Go on, don't pull any punches. You see a thin-haired (that's being generous), somewhat-less-than-graceful, middle-aged man who's no page out of *GQ*. (Okay, okay, maybe I could pass as one of those "before" ads for some product or another, but you get the point.) And yet what you see is about all I've got. Believe it or not, but here I am, Mr. Ripley, making a very nice living in a business where style counts a whole lot more than substance, where what you say doesn't matter nearly so much as how you say it (and how you look at the time), where your IQ won't take you to dinner if your "Q" score can't pick up the check.

I've beaten the odds, I'm proud to say, although I'm not too proud to admit I don't exactly know how or why. Maybe it has something to do with one of my most endearing qualities (or my most annoying, depending on whom you talk to): I don't give up easily. I'm a relentless son-of-a-gun. If at first I don't succeed . . . well, you know the rest. Maybe it's just dumb luck. But whatever it is, the hairs on my neck (what hairs there are) still stand on end in celebration whenever one of my impossible dreams comes true, and they do their thing for other impossible dreamers, too.

In fact, my smart money is forever riding on the other folks who've come into this thing with much longer odds than mine, the folks whose hopes and dreams seem, well, impossible. I'm faced with only small handicaps compared with the setbacks facing some of the brave and courageous people I've met between our coasts. Really, my heart is lifted like you wouldn't believe by some of the stories I hear, and it's broken by some of the others. Smooth moves don't mean diddly to a young woman who grew up in the shadow of leukemia; an out-of-step wardrobe is no great shakes to a veteran who's lost three of his limbs in the Vietnam War; a shiny bald head is no big deal to an independent young woman with cerebral palsy; and a bulging waistline is neither here, there, nor anywhere to a midwestern artist who, legally and almost literally, can't see a blessed thing. These are the people you'll read about in this chapter, and your hairs can stand on end along with mine as their impossible dreams come true all over again.

These spirited and determined people have hurdled great obstacles to lead rich and productive lives. You'll pardon the poker metaphor here, but I'm on a roll with this gambling thing and I just can't resist: the cards may have been stacked against these brave folks, but each of them has called life's bluff and come up a winner. Their courage is encouraging and, I hope, inspiring.

Take heart, and read on.

* *

Kim Hill joins in the dedication ceremonies for a new Ronald McDonald House with a mutual friend.

"SOMEBODY MUST HAVE BIG PLANS FOR ME"

★ KIM HILL

San Juan Capistrano, California

Kim Hill is an inspiration, in every sense of the word. She is an inspiration to anyone diagnosed with acute lymphatic leukemia (or with any type of cancer), having beaten the long odds of the disease as a small child. And, equally important, she is the inspiration for the successful development over the past dozen or so years of the more than one hundred Ronald McDonald Houses established with leading hospitals around the country.

Were it not for Kim Hill and everything she suffered (and

75

oh, I wouldn't wish that kind of suffering on my worst enemy), it is entirely possible that the Ronald McDonald House program would never have gotten off the ground, that the parents and families of children with serious and terminal illnesses would be without the safe and peaceful and convenient haven provided by the halfway houses. "In some ways I'm glad I was sick," says Kim, now twenty. "I know that's the biggest cliché in the world, but it's true. I didn't at all enjoy being sick. It was one of the worst experiences in my life, actually it was the worst, by far. But I'm glad it was me who got sick because so much good has been able to come from it."

So much good was able to come from it because Kim's father was being paid to catch a football for a living, as a tight end for the Philadelphia Eagles, when Kim was diagnosed with leukemia at the age of three. (The complete story of the development of the Ronald McDonald Houses will be told elsewhere in these pages, when I introduce you to Jim Murray, the former general manager of the Eagles and a kindhearted individual if ever there was one.) And as Kim was receiving experimental treatments in the very early 1970s, she had the entire Eagles organization and what seemed like the whole city of Philadelphia in her corner. I entered the picture much later, but I hear stories of how everybody rallied around Kim and, soon, others like her, and I feel grateful for the chance to have been associated in some small way with the project.

"It was absolutely awful," Kim remembers of the chemotherapy and radiation treatments she was undergoing as a three- and four-year-old. "I never really felt good when I was little. I remember most of it pretty vividly. And what I remember most of all is I was always in some kind of pain, or terribly nauseated, or being stuck with big, long needles. But the whole time I really didn't understand what was happening to me, and part of me felt that my parents were doing this to me on purpose. I just couldn't understand why they were doing this to me, but they couldn't tell a four-year-old girl that if she didn't go and have the treatments, she would probably die. How do you tell something like that to a little girl?"

Kim remembers the difficulties her parents had in learning

to help Kim cope with the disease, in learning how much a frightened and confused little girl was able to understand. "I was the most spoiled kid in the world," Kim says now with the benefit of hindsight. "I was given constant attention, and I was given everything I could ever want. I guess that was one way my parents found to make it up to me, to make all the pain and hurt go away. The trouble is, when I went into remission nobody knew how to act around me. As I got older and it wasn't like I was going to die or anything, I was still conditioned to expect everything. But they were trying to reverse the way they were treating me. That's a hard message for a kid to understand, you know: If you're going to die, we'll treat you special and give you anything you want, but if you're not going to die, then we'll treat you like everybody else."

Kim's on to something here. I've noticed, over the years, that parents just don't know how to act when their kids are hospitalized. I'm not saying that Kim's folks did anything they shouldn't have done, not at all, only that most parents, in general, don't know which buttons to let their kids push to get what they want, that sort of thing. It's a tough problem, and there's no place to learn to handle it except through trial by fire. I listen to Kim relive those confusing and frightening times, and it breaks my heart, but I'm also glad she's able to recall and articulate her feelings in a way that will hopefully help others through similar hard times.

It wasn't until she was a teenager that Kim finally made sense of what she and her family went through (she also has two younger sisters), that she was able to put the entire ordeal into some sort of perspective. "I was watching a movie on television," she says, "about a young kid who had cancer, when it finally hit me what had happened to me. Oh, I always knew in some sense what went on, but it didn't seem real or tangible, you know, not until I saw something similar played out on T.V. The whole thing wasn't real to me."

But Kim's battle with leukemia was very real, and during the war she missed out on huge chunks of her little girlhood. "I was always being taken out of school," she says, "always in the hospital, or sick at home. I never really had friends when I was little because I was out of school so much, and

when I was there I always got the feeling, you know, everyone was looking at me, or pointing at me. There were always
these articles about me, or about the Ronald McDonald
House, and people knew who I was.

"Everybody at the hospital I always went to, they all knew
me, the doctors and the nurses, everybody. I remember when
it came time for me to stop treatment, I was torn, I really was.
I had more friends there than I had at school, and I was sad
to leave them. I remember telling everybody, 'I'm gonna
miss you, but I'm really not.' I didn't know what to think."

But Kim has put all that behind her now, and she's getting
on with the rest of her life. After a couple of stops and starts
at colleges in her area, she is finally ready to get her higher
education into full swing, this time with an eye toward a
career in sociology or psychology. She's spent the past few
summers working at a California camp for kids with cancer—
Camp Good Times—where she is able to stand as living,
breathing proof that you can come out on the winning end of
even the worst type of cancer; it is when she's working with
these campers, Kim says, that it dawns on her how lucky
she's been.

Kim still hears from friendly strangers around the country
who first became interested in her struggle through the
media accounts of the Ronald McDonald House story and
legend and who write to see how she's progressing. "Parents
are always coming up to me and saying things like 'What is
my daughter feeling right now? What is she going
through?'" Kim tells me. "It's hard to know what to say, but
I try to help them, I try to tell them something they'll take
comfort in, and I'm glad they're asking me. I know my parents would have loved to ask the same things of someone
who'd been through what I've now been through."

Over the years, Kim has traveled extensively on the part of
the Ronald McDonald Houses, and everywhere she goes she
is given the royal treatment. We bumped into each other
recently in New Hyde Park, New York, at the opening of the
one hundredth Ronald McDonald House, a significant record
of achievement and a fitting, working monument to Kim's
proud struggle. I can still remember looking over at her during the opening ceremonies and watching her absorb the

impact and influence of her childhood suffering; I could see in her eyes the proud knowledge that, whatever it may have cost her and her family (and it did indeed cost them), her illness counted for something.

"I feel like I was put on this place for a purpose," she said after the dedication. "After everything I've been through, I'm still here. Somebody must have big plans for me."

★ ★

"Really, as an artist I'm at an advantage."—Scott Nelson in his studio.

THE ART OF LIVING

★ **SCOTT NELSON**
Minneapolis, Minnesota

When he was twenty-five years old, Scott Nelson had lost nearly 80 percent of his vision. He was also driving a car and functioning in ways that seemed, for lack of a better word, normal, certainly in ways that did not seem visually impaired. Scott Nelson had no real notion he was suffering from something called retinitis pigmentosa, or that he was legally blind.

"I had no idea," he says now from his studio in Minneapolis, where he works in welded metal sculpture and in plastic and wax to achieve some of the most challenging and exciting pieces I've ever seen. "Somehow I had developed these uncanny ways to get around, to the extent that I really didn't know I was losing my sight. I knew enough to know I was having some vision problems, enough to take myself to the doctor to check it out, but not enough to think it was anything serious, certainly not enough to think I was legally blind." It's amazing to me the way the body is able to adapt, to come up with enough ways of coping and adjusting so that someone like Scott can function productively under those kinds of conditions. I've seen it throughout my professional life with my friend and partner, Ed Walker, who is blind (you'll get a chance to read about him a little bit later in the book), and I'm sure I will forever marvel at the way people like Ed and Scott are able to compensate for the things they haven't got.

Scott, now thirty-nine, has since lost another 10 percent of his vision (as if you can actually pin a number on what he has or what he doesn't have), but he is still able to conduct his life without noticeable interruption; he can no longer drive, and he has trouble negotiating dark hallways and passages, but these days he focuses on what he can do.

And what he can do, still, is see, and he can see things in new and exciting ways he had never thought possible. As an artist, Scott has redirected his handicap to where he has overcome it; in many ways he looks on his visual impairment as an asset in his work and as a means to a clearer understanding and appreciation of life's big picture. "I should really be totally blind three times over by now," he says. "The medical authorities, everyone I've been to, they're stumped. I'm not supposed to be able to see a thing."

Scott says that when he was first diagnosed fifteen years ago, he was told to expect to lose his sight completely within a few years. "Right away I had this compulsion to do as much as I could while I could still see," he remembers. "I had this compulsion to create as much as I possibly could, to travel the world as much as I possibly could, to see as much as I could, everything.

"But after a while that kind of compulsion can become paralyzing. You can't do anything with it. It took me about a year, and then I realized I could still achieve what I wanted to achieve, even though I would continue to lose my vision. I've been lucky—doctors tell me I'm lucky I can still see as well as I do—but it is something I have to deal with and confront every day. Part of me is still hanging in the denial phase, which I guess is part of the process of losing anything."

Scott's loss, to hear him tell it, has also been his gain, and it has clearly been to the gain of other visually impaired artists around the country. Since 1980 he has worked to establish a touring art exhibit featuring works by blind or visually impaired artists, as an investigation into an artist's unique inner vision, and today his "The Art of the Eye" exhibition has gained national prominence with its collection of over fifty works by twenty-four contemporary visually impaired artists. "We're not like other handicapped-artist exhibitions," Scott explains of "The Art of the Eye," "which most times simply, and nobly, provide exposure opportunities for handicapped artists. We're out for something much more. We're out to affect people's feelings, their perceptions, and we hope to learn more about the role of vision perception in the minds of artists who can't use their eyes."

One of the things Scott tries to do in his work is help people see things the way he does, and for the most part he sees things in a way that can best be described as tunnel vision. Place your hands, palms facing palms, at the far corners of your eyes, and then draw them slowly toward each other, and you'll get a better idea of what Scott can and can't see. I've tried it, and I'm all the more impressed with what Scott's been able to do. It's like going through life with blinders on, and it seems to me it must be one of the most frustrating experiences imaginable, particularly if you were once fully sighted.

Scott can also tinker with various sighting instruments to allow fully sighted people to share the experience of tunnel vision, duplicating the effect of reduced peripheral vision and depth perception. He also works in something called "sun cartography," a performance art medium in which he sets up a performance event lasting from sunup to sundown, using the movements of the sun to accentuate and highlight the piece; I've never seen his work in this area but hope someday to have the chance. To a weatherman like myself, the use of the sun in an evolving work of art sounds fascinating.

Almost all the artists in "The Art of the Eye" have had significant successes on their own, Scott Nelson included, with work that is appreciated not merely for the fact that it was created by a visually impaired person, but for itself alone. Many are represented in leading art museums around the country, alongside the works of sighted artists, and many have been featured in prestigious one-man and one-woman shows. "We want people to come away from 'The Art of the Eye' and not take their sight for granted," he says. "We want them to be able to see the world through our eyes. In walking away from the exhibit, I kind of hope people drop whatever sympathy they've had for me or the other artists and replace it with empathy and understanding."

The eye-opening success and achievement enjoyed by Scott and his colleagues is not without precedent in the annals of art history; artists such as Rembrandt, Mary Cassatt, Monet, Renoir, El Greco, Domiere, and Van Gogh are said to have suffered from some type of visual impairment; Degas is said to have created his best work when he was legally blind. (There are other examples, too, dozens of them, but I'm not what you would call an art expert—as far as I'm concerned, you're a pro if you can stay between the lines on the color-by-numbers set—and these are the only names I recognized as Scott rattled off a surprisingly long list.)

"I think our exhibit raises powerful questions about the validity and necessity of sight," Scott says, "at least the need for perfect, twenty-twenty vision. Much of our most creative and dramatic artwork, throughout art history, has come from visually impaired artists. When sight fails the brain kicks in and provides compensatory images that sometimes exceed what the eye can see. We like to joke that other artists will become so envious of our perspective that they'll pluck out their eyes. Really, as an artist, I'm at an advantage."

I guess what Scott Nelson and his "Art of the Eye" exhibit teach us is that the eyes don't necessarily have it, that when we lose pieces of ourselves, we build and draw on other aspects and abilities to compensate, that even the darkest cloud has some kind of silver lining. How remarkable our world must look through Scott Nelson's eyes and through the eyes of his colleagues. How remarkable indeed.

★ ★

"I've always believed in me."—
Tommy Clack with his wife and son.

STARTING OVER

★ TOMMY CLACK
Stone Mountain, Georgia

Tommy Clack is a Vietnam War veteran, although he doesn't think of himself as a war hero. "The guys who didn't come home, all the dead and the missing, they're the real heroes of that war," he says. "They're the people who made the supreme sacrifice."

But whether he thinks so or not, Tommy's story is a heroic one indeed. He lost both his legs, all of his right arm, and part of his shoulder, in a battle at a place the soldiers called the Angel's Wing, so named for the way the land jutted out into the water toward Saigon. Tommy, an enlisted man on his second tour of duty, was stationed there as a captain in the army's Twenty-fifth Division, serving as a forward observer on this mission, and it was his job to call out the plane and artillery strikes to his troops.

He remembers the incident vividly, and his recollection is haunting: "There was lots of incoming fire, and I got hit by something. I still don't know what it was, but all of a sudden it tore off three of my limbs. I was conscious through the whole thing. In the movie *Butch Cassidy and the Sundance Kid*, there was a scene when they loaded a train with too much dynamite, and everything was in super, super slow motion. That's what it was like for me. Everything was happening slow as possible, really super slow. I don't think I was in shock. I knew exactly what was happening, what had happened. I saw both legs gone. I was tore open. I could see my right lung pumping. I lay back down to die."

In a way, that's what he did. "I was considered technically dead," Tommy says in a rich southern accent, made richer with a life that has been given back to him, "but obviously it wasn't my time to go." Tommy's insight as one of the few who have survived what you might call a clinical death has been sought by doctors and scientists and social historians, and he does report a so-called near death experience. "I was very definitely removed from my body," he says matter-of-factly, almost detached. "I watched them administer to my wounds, and I communicated with some of the men who'd served under my command, some of the ones I'd put in body bags. They tried to get me to go where they were going, but like I said, I guess it wasn't my time. It was a very real experience for me."

But even a near death experience could not prepare Tommy for the life he would lead as a triple amputee. He returned to the States in June of 1969, and he spent the next twenty-two months in hospitals here, during which time he underwent some thirty operations. "I had to relearn everything," he says now. "I had to learn how to sit up, how to crawl, how to walk, how to dress, everything." But he managed. He overcame his handicaps and slowly and painstakingly went about the business, he says, "of becoming a functioning human being again."

During his rehabilitation, Tommy was clearly aware of his changing situation, but the impact of the war itself wasn't really brought home to him until he saw a *Life* magazine photo essay, featuring 333 pictures of 333 soldiers who died during the last week in May 1969. "That was just around the time of my accident," he recalls, "and I knew forty-seven of the guys personally. That hit me more than any other thing, really hit me. For some reason *Life* magazine made the war more real than it ever could be on television or in the newspapers. In a sense it was more real than it was when we were over there."

Patriotism pulses strong through Tommy Clack's veins, as it does through mine, but I have to guess that Tommy's just a touch more patriotic than most people. For a long time after he returned home, he traveled the country, to high schools and college campuses, talking about his undying American spirit, about volunteerism, about the red, white, and blue, about a war he desperately believed in. "I got hit with more than my share of rotten eggs and tomatoes," Tommy says. "Lots of people didn't agree with my viewpoint, but that's what makes this country so wonderful. That's one of the things I was fighting for, the right for people to have different opinions." I don't want to get into a long discussion here on the justification for our involvement in the Vietnam War—it's not the appropriate time or place—but I have to admire Tommy's solid, unflagging belief in what he was doing over there, in what he's been doing since he got back.

Tommy's travels got him involved in many local civic groups, and he eventually rose through the ranks of Georgia's Jay Cees, one of the more dynamic youth groups in the country, to become the organization's state president. He lent his energies and his speaking talents to political campaigns. "A lot of what I was doing at the time was for show," Tommy concedes. "People came out to hear a disabled Vietnam veteran, they didn't come out to hear me, but I have no problem with that as long as it's helpful to one other person. I think I filled a lot of people's equal-opportunity requirements when I was out looking for a job. They could say they'd interviewed a disabled veteran and then give the job to somebody else." After his return home, until 1979, Tommy lived off his

VA disability compensation, which amounted to about $700 each month.

That year, though, he was offered a job as staff assistant to the director of the VA Medical Center, Atlanta, and ever since he's been serving as a sort of administrative liaison for veterans in his area. "I've been putting my mouth in gear," he says. "I may have lost my legs and my right arm, but my brain's intact, and my mouth works, and my left arm and shoulder keep me functioning. I can swim, and I can still hunt and fish, and I can play football and basketball with the kids in the schools. I can tie my own ties and button my own buttons. I can do everything I used to do except run." He can even drive a car, with a special device attached to his shoulder and torso that allows him to work the brake and gas pedals.

After a few years on the job, Tommy met a young woman at the hospital, and the two became the best of friends. "I had been dating ever since my accident," he tells, "but this was something different, something special." The best friends were married nearly four years ago, and the couple has a one-year-old son. "Everything else about my life is normal," Tommy says. "I don't think of myself as anything special, as any sort of exceptional person. What I've achieved I've achieved not because of my accident or despite my accident, but because I've always been an achiever. I've always believed in me."

Tommy, as you may have guessed from his Butch Cassidy reference earlier, is a movie buff, although he isn't entirely pleased with the way the Vietnam War is often portrayed on the big screen. "If you can actually believe what we're asked to in some of these movies, then we would have won this war in its first year," he insists. "What are people gonna think twenty years from now if all that's left is what Hollywood's given us? What is the record gonna show for my son when he grows up? There are no real Rambos.

"The true history of Vietnam has yet to be written, but when it is I want it to go down showing that we were right. I believed in what we were doing there, and if I hadn't gotten injured on my second tour, I would have gone back for a third. Even knowing what would happen to me, I'd go back and do it again. I firmly believe in the long run that the war and all of us who fought in it will be vindicated, that the record will show our involvement there was just and noble. It may sound cruel, but all this talk about how Vietnam vets are struggling to make their way back in society is exaggerated. I know it's not popular to say this, but Vietnam vets are no different from the veterans of any other war; the only difference is that no other war was seen on television at dinner every night.

"Ninety-five percent of all Vietnam vets, I would guess, are making positive contributions to their communities. Outwardly they show no signs of their involvement in the war, but inwardly, I'm sure many of them still suffer. I know I still do. I still wake up some nights in a cold sweat, but I don't think that makes me sick, I don't think that makes me troubled. I remember, that's all, and I hope I always do remember. I think it keeps me sane, remembering. When you get shot at, you always remember it."

Tommy says he doesn't regret that there was no hero's welcome on his return. "Like I said, I'm no hero," he insists again. "Besides, I don't know what a hero's welcome is. We've given ourselves our own welcome back. I think the attitude of the country is changing. Twenty-eight of our fifty states have already erected monuments on behalf of those who died in the war, and more are coming." Tommy, incidentally, was instrumental in making Georgia the first state to dedicate a statue to veterans of the Vietnam War, back in 1979.

"We've come a long way since the war ended in 1975," Tommy says, "but we've still got a long way to go. In a sense the Vietnam War will never be over until the last veteran dies, and for that you're looking a long way down the road."

★ ★

"I can handle almost anything."
—Julie Weissman.

CALIFORNIA, HERE SHE COMES!

★ JULIE WEISSMAN
Berkeley, California

Every once in a long while I come across an exceptional individual whose triumphs and accomplishments make me feel good all over.

Julie Weissman is one of those rare finds. Just to look at this college student's curriculum vitae you wouldn't think there was anything extraordinary about this extraordinary young woman. Oh, she's bright and she's pretty and she's active in all sorts of campus activities, but that alone doesn't tell the whole story.

You see, Julie was born with cerebral palsy, a disorder that results from damage to the developing brain and that typically affects the ability to control voluntary muscle activity. For Julie, it's meant a lifetime struggle just to speak or eat or move from here to there. Her speech is dysarthric, which basically means it's not easy for her to get her mouth to say what she wants you to hear; she communicates slowly and with what seems like great effort. Her muscle activity is clinically described as athetoid, which means Julie can move her body the way she wants only with great difficulty and limited success. She gets around in a wheelchair by pushing herself with her feet or with a motorized assist; she can't walk, feed, or bathe herself, and she needs somebody's help to get up each morning and to go to bed each night.

Yet like nearly every other student in her high school graduating class a few years back, Julie anxiously looked forward to an out-of-town college experience. She chose the University of California at Berkeley, nearly a continent away from her parents' home on Long Island, partly because it could boast one of the leading disabled students programs in the country and partly because it was so far away from home. "That's what I like about it," Julie says of the distance from a hometown that didn't exactly make growing up all that easy; she tells me now that she had no close friends from her public high school, that the other kids weren't nearly as nice or understanding as they could have been, that she was often excluded even from routine social activities because she was, well, different. "My mother and I went to look at Berkeley, and I loved it," she says. "The people there are not at all like the people from where I grew up, and the whole campus, the whole city, was easy to move around in. My father wasn't exactly thrilled. He wanted me to be closer to home, but Berkeley was my first choice."

You wouldn't think growing up with cerebral palsy would be easy, but in Julie's case it came with more problems than you might expect. In the first place, she didn't go to a public school until high school, which meant she was frustrated through several years of disabled students programs in which her classmates were not only physically disabled but often intellectually limited as well. Julie's smarter than I am, if you want an unbiased opinion (most folks are, come to think of it), but for a long time the distinction between physical and intellectual abilities had not been properly made, and there she was, stuck in an environment that didn't allow her to realize anything near her potential. She was being held back on account of her disability, yet when she finally did talk her way into the public school system, well, then came the hard part: "The other kids were cruel," she recalls. "How would you like to be sitting with a group of kids your own age and have them talking about a sweet sixteen party you're not invited to? They would talk about things like that right in front of me, like I wasn't even there." Julie's classmates obviously thought she was too different to be included among them, and that kind of rejection is awful tough to shoulder for any teenager.

And on top of the heartless behavior of the other students, Julie says the high school administration wasn't exactly responsive to her particular needs. "I was the only disabled person in the school," she says, "and there was never any acknowledgment that I was not like other people." Teachers wouldn't make it easy for Julie, an honors student, to take exams (she had to dictate her response during the same time frame as the rest of the class), and though she wasn't looking for any special treatment, Julie doesn't think she was always given a fair shake. "If it's easier for you to type, why should you dictate?" she wants to know. "Disabled people are not like nondisabled people, so why should we be asked to do things in the same way? But I told myself I had to be successful for the other disabled students who would come after me. My attitude was, I have to get through this, and then when I get to college things will be different." I guess what we can all learn from Julie's high school days is that too often we look on disabled people as different in ways in which they're really the same (as in a social context, with her classmates), while at the same time we look at them as the same in ways in which they're really different (as in an academic context, with the school being unable to adapt to Julie's abilities).

Things were different when she got to Berkeley, much different. For one thing, professors let her take exams any way she pleased, and more often than not she chooses to type out her answers on her Compaq computer. She types with her toes, by the way, because she can control them far better than she can control her fingers. (She's been able to do so much with the help of her computer, she feels she'd be lost without it, so she's bought a second one for use as a backup whenever the first breaks down; so far, wouldn't you know it, she hasn't had to take the thing out of the box.) For another, she made friends for the first time in her life with people her own age who were not disabled. Good friends.

Leaving home for college is difficult enough without the handicaps Julie brings to the picture. She'd never lived away from home before, on her own, but she wasn't afraid to charter unknown territory. That's one of the things that so impresses me about this remarkable young woman; her fierce independence would be a wonderful thing to see in any person her age. Her first year at school, Julie lived in a dorm with both disabled and nondisabled students. "A lot of the other schools with disabled students programs have what I call 'crip' dorms," Julie says, "where you're living just with other disabled students. I didn't want to be isolated like that." There was a twenty-four-hour attendant on duty for emergencies, and the school helped out with part-time attendants until Julie could hire her own. She now employs a staff of eight attendants who help her with errands, chores, and house cleaning and with her general care and feeding.

She lived in a single room her freshman year, without any of the pleasures or headaches of having a roommate, because the small dormitory rooms could barely accommodate Julie, her two computers, her two wheelchairs, and other assorted equipment. "I take up a lot of room," she says. (So do I.)

In addition to assisting with attendant care, Berkeley and the state of California also subsidize the hiring of secretaries, note takers, lab assistants, anybody Julie might need to assist her in her studies. Including blind and learning-disabled students, the school's disabled students program is some three hundred strong, although when I last spoke with Julie it was in danger of losing some of its funding. That would be a shame, really, because nowhere in my travels have I seen a more worthwhile, productive, or cost-efficient program to assist disabled individuals in search of a higher education. They've even got an on-site repair shop to handle equipment (mostly wheelchair) breakdowns, which will give you an idea to what lengths the school goes to cover all the bases. "One year I spent half my time in the repair shop," Julie jokes. "I don't know what I would have done without it."

Outside of school, Julie's interests are varied. She keeps a daily journal, and lately she's been very active in the campus chapter of the United Jewish Appeal. In fact, she was recently named to chair the campus UJA campaign, a task that's got her pretty excited. Her position as chair brought with it a trip to Israel with a UJA leadership group. "It's the first time I've been in a leadership position over nondisabled people," she tells of her UJA responsibilities. "After a while I got scared about it. I wondered, Is it fair for me to take this position? How am I going to get people to work with me if they're scared of the way I look or the way I speak? But then my rabbi told me, 'Julie, since when have you used your disability as an excuse?' and he was right. I didn't realize that's what I was doing." In an article she wrote for a United Cerebral Palsy publication, Julie gets to the heart of what she's learned at Berkeley and through her work with UJA: "Now I'm judged by what I do, not how I look or speak."

At twenty-one, Julie admits she doesn't know what the future holds for her beyond Berkeley, and like any student she's a little bit frightened about what lies ahead. Right now she's thinking of a career in education or in counseling; already she's begun teaching word processing to a disabled junior high school student, as part of an internship program set up with the school. "I don't know how realistic that is," Julie says, "but right now that's what I'm working toward. Maybe I'll just hide out in graduate school for a few years. You know, I'm going crazy right now because I have a friend back at home, she's twenty-six and she's in a wheelchair and she's still living at home. Her parents won't let her come out, they're very protective of her, they're overprotective, but what's going to happen when they die? What's going to happen to her? I know for me that no matter what the future holds, I can handle almost anything. I have a full life now, and I'll have a full life when I graduate. I'm worried about things, sure. Who isn't? But I can take care of myself, I know that."

No doubt about it.

GOD, it makes me feel good to introduce you to these brave folks, proud for the chance to include them here. I'm overcome by what they've overcome. That's a nice line, an easy line, but it says it all for me.

Sometimes I wonder how I'd hold up under their kind of extraordinary circumstances, if I'd even hold up at all. I do know that whenever life takes an unexpected turn, as it no doubt will, I'll be looking to Kim Hill, Scott Nelson, Tommy Clack, Julie Weissman, and others like them for inspiration. I'll be looking to follow their lead and make great strides through little steps.

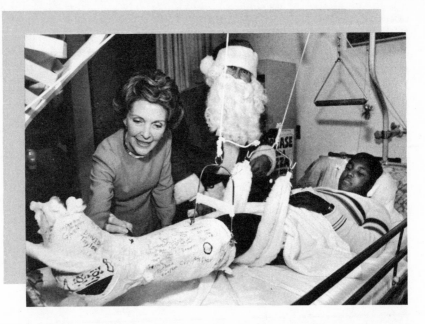

Who's that good-looking Santa Claus paying a visit with the First Lady?

6 It's Beginning to Look a Lot Like Christmas

FIRST things first: Thanksgiving is my favorite holiday. What a way to start a chapter on the beauty of the Christmas spirit, but hey—I call 'em like I see 'em! Look, I'm a Pilgrim at heart, and Thanksgiving just gets me all warm and tingly and all kinds of wonderful inside. It reminds me of my grandparents' farm, and it's forever associated with the smells and colors of fall, my favorite season. Also, Thanksgiving means food, lots of food, and most of you already know how I feel about that.

Okay, so these are a few of my favorite things, but what about my second-favorite things? Well, my second-favorite things are pretty much all Christmas-related, which kind of fills the space between Thanksgiving and Christmas with all sorts of good things great and small. Chestnuts, feel free to roast upon my open fire any old time you please; Jack Frost, take a bite out of this old honker! Ho, ho, ho, 'tis the season to be jolly, and for an all-around jolly character like yours truly, Christmas 'tis a special time of year. My favorite kind of folks are those who overflow with healthy doses of the season's good cheer. I guess you could say I'm overflowing with the stuff, too, and to look at me you might think I've had second helpings.

If you'll permit me a serious note, Christmas is the centerpiece of the Christian faith. For me it is forever associated with the Christmas story, with the birth of Christ. I look at the way Christmas has been processed and commercialized over the years, and it doesn't really bother me, so long as we don't lose sight of the true meaning of the holiday, so long as we don't let Madison Avenue get in the way of the man upstairs. A special feeling permeates the air during the holiday seasons, and I have to think it has something to do with what Christmas means, or at least with what it's supposed to mean. I think the good cheer, warm spirits, and glad tidings rub off on people. How else do you explain why nearly every year it seems a terrorist releases a long-held hostage just before Christmas? How else do you explain why sometimes bitter negotiations are often resolved amicably before the end of the year? How else do you explain why good deeds come in bigger bunches during the Christmas season than at any other time of year? Are people capitalizing on the holiday's public relations value, or is there really a spillover of peace-on-earth-goodwill-toward-man feeling that gets in the way of everything else?

Oh, I don't know. But what I do know is Christmas means all things to all people. For many of us, Christmas means Santa Claus, in some form or another. A very clever man down in Wheeling, West Virginia, once told me he'd discovered the true three stages of man: the first, he said, comes in childhood, when you still believe in Santa; the second occurs with skepticism, when the image and ideal of the Christmas spirit goes the way of the tooth fairy and Tinker Bell; by the

The ghost of Christmas past.

third stage, my Wheeling sage advised, man has come full circle, to where he dresses up as Kris Kringle, and I'm happy as a bowlful of egg nog to be right smack dab in the middle of this stage in my development.

I'll admit it, I'm built like Santa, or at least the way we imagine Santa, and I've been borrowing the good man's clothes since I was fifteen years old. Of course, I didn't always fit the suit like I do now. Used to be I'd have to stuff a few pillows under my belt, but these days I'm my own pillow. In fact, last time I put on my red suit it was a touch tight around the middle, and this was without the benefit of artificial padding. (Remind me to make a note of that for my New Year's resolutions.) But no matter what I've looked like on the outside, people for some reason have always thought of me as a Santa Claus on the inside. I've been typecast, because really, during the rest of the year, I live my life like a Santa Claus in a seersucker suit.

Everywhere I've ever worked, I've been asked to play the

part, and since 1973 I've been doing my thing for the National Park Service and the annual lighting of the National Christmas Tree on the White House lawn. It always gets to me, the White House Christmas ceremony. They've got fifty small trees, representing the fifty states, and the huge national tree; to round out the picture they've got honest-to-goodness reindeer, a smoking Yule log, and a military band trumpeting out some Christmas carols. It's hard to believe that with trimmings like these, they never had a Santa on hand until 1973, but I'm glad that when they finally did get around to putting Santa on the guest list, someone thought to invite me.

But enough about my soaring Christmas spirits. For now, leave some milk and cookies under the tree for the good folks you'll meet below, folks who've turned on an abundance of good cheer and glad tidings to build a life where it's Christmas morning all year long.

★ ★

LIGHTING UP THE WINTER NIGHT

★ RANDY WORLS
Wheeling, West Virginia

My friend Randy Worls has got his backyard wired for Christmas like you wouldn't believe. He's got more than half a million individual lights strung up in fine and fancy patterns designed by award-winning artists, the whole thing covering more than three hundred acres of beautifully landscaped property and powered over its fifty-day winter run by more than 1.2 million watts of electricity.

Actually, Randy's so-called backyard isn't his alone, it belongs to his hometown community of Wheeling. As general manager of the Wheeling Park Commission, Randy lives on the grounds of the fifteen-hundred-acre Oglebay Park, a wonderful vacation and recreation facility and the only self-

*Standing in front
of Willard the
Snowman with
Randy Worls (left)
and lighting
designer Bob
Otten.*

sustaining major park system in the United States. And since Christmas 1985, Randy has helped to launch a year-round effort to turn the park and its on-site hotel and resort complex into a veritable winter wonderland with one of the largest-known Christmas lights displays in the country.

I had the honor last year of being invited to help kick off Oglebay's second annual Festival of Lights, and let me tell you this place and this display are all kinds of wonderful. The entire effect is hypnotic, the way the lights spread out before you, with flooded landscape vistas, light-enhanced historical buildings, and acres upon acres of captivating candy-colored displays. On a clear night, my favorite weatherman permitting, the festival sparks a special magic in the night sky, lighting the entire park in majestic and wonderful splendor. Unfortunately, the fog was so thick on the night of my visit you couldn't see past the bridge of your nose, and because of the weather we had to cancel plans for a special helicopter ride for an aerial view of the lighted park. I hope to schedule a return trip to experience the full effect of the place, but I saw enough on that first visit to know that the folks in Wheeling have got something special with this winter festival, and the someone special they've got to thank for it goes by the name of Randy Worls.

A quiet and unassuming man of forty-eight, Randy is a sixth-generation Wheelingite who has spurred his hometown into a resurgence of sorts. Two years ago, he got together with a friend of his, Ross Felton, thinking the two of them could help chase away each other's winter doldrums. Ross operates WWVA, a fifty-thousand-watt radio station that sponsors a program called Jamboree USA, which each weekend attracts some five thousand visitors to the Wheeling area. The trouble was, during the month of December, the Jamboree was only attracting about two hundred folks per show, and the lodge at Randy's Oglebay resort was only operating at about 10 percent occupancy. What, the two men wanted to know, would keep people coming to Wheeling in the winter months in numbers consistent with their rest-of-the-year statistics?

It wasn't exactly like a light bulb flicked on over their heads with inspiration, let alone a string of Christmas lights. "We hired a tour bus consultant after our brainstorming session," Randy recalls, "and we asked him where most operators sent their buses during the winter. He told us most tour operators in the Northeast run trips to Niagara Falls that time of year, not to see the falls, but to see their lights display. So we thought to ourselves, Hey, that's something we can do here. We can put on as good a show. We're not above plagiarism at Oglebay, so we took a cue from Niagara Falls."

Word of mouth eventually put Randy in touch with Dick Bosch, a world-renowned lighting artist from the Netherlands who had previously bathed the Taj Mahal in India, the Parthenon in Athens, and the Great Pyramids in Egypt with his multicolored vision. Bosch was intrigued by Randy's idea and eventually teamed with local design consultant Bob Otten to shape and craft Wheeling's Festival of Lights. Randy's dream of launching his own festival based on the successful Niagara Falls light show was a giant step closer to reality.

"Our festival is a lot different from the Niagara Falls show," Randy says. "The display is designed to be seen from your car. You know, most of the time in December we have pretty inclement weather, and we wanted to design the thing so people could still enjoy it without being too uncomfortable outdoors. We couldn't really have something where you had to walk around to see it, like they do up there." Last year's festival included an exhibit the size of a football field commemorating the twelve days of Christmas, with eight-foot maids a-milking, pipers piping, you know, the whole bit. It also featured a unique, hand-crafted nativity scene—I believe it's one of the largest in the country—with life-size figurines and a giant menorah. There were dozens of other exhibits, too, but the highlight of the show for me had to be a thirty-foot happy-go-lightly fellow named Willard the Snowman. (I wonder where they came up with that one?) Take my word for it, you haven't known true Christmas cheer and excitement until you've been immortalized in one of Oglebay's Festival of Lights displays.

By all accounts, the Festival of Lights has been a blazing success. The display was produced at a total cost of $550,000 during its first two years, and Randy figures the business generated by tourists and local enthusiasts returned that investment to the community several fold. "The infusion of dollars into our business community has been tremendous," he reports. "The Niagara Falls festival returns about $15 million in generated business in a five-year period, and we launched our festival hoping to bring in $7 million over a similar span. We thought we were being conservative in our estimate, but we're already ahead of schedule." Before I even had a chance to flick the switch to light the second annual display—with an able assist from West Virginia Governor Arch Moore—Randy figured there were more than 500 tour buses booked for visits during that Christmas season, and the park system was estimating a month-long traffic jam of more than 125,000 cars carrying more than 500,000 people.

But Randy has done more than light up the once dim prospects of Wheeling with his inspiration. He has lit up the area's winter sky with hope and good cheer. Long a center of steel, coal, and blown-glass production, Wheeling has survived a series of setbacks in those industries and the big-hearted people there are rebuilding their proud community. Wheeling was recently named the safest city in the country (they have the lowest crime rate), and the quality of life in Wheeling and surrounding areas is judged by the locals to be about the best you can find. They rolled out the red carpet when I came to town, so it's kind of hard for me to judge the quality of life firsthand, but I have a hunch they roll out the red carpet for just about everybody down in Wheeling; it's that kind of place.

"We're experiencing a totally upbeat and uplifting situation here," Randy assesses, "and the Festival of Lights is only a part of it. But the festival is a good example of how people here are working together to make this a better place to live. Beginning each January, we have students from the vocational schools here volunteering to help lay the groundwork for the next year's festival. Our exhibits are built and donated by local artists and craftsmen. A good portion of our funding comes from the private sector. The whole thing, what with the planning and everything, is a year-round effort, and we get help from an awful lot of people."

Randy is the kind of guy who likes to deflect a lot of credit for the resounding success enjoyed by the festival, and he is reluctant to heap any of the glory on himself. But, he admits, it is hard to shake a feeling of personal pride when he looks at the festival in its full glow. "On a very personal level, the festival is one of the greatest thrills of my life," he lets on. "From a business standpoint, yes, it's been tremendously successful in revitalizing this area, but from a personal standpoint, I can't tell you how rewarding it is to go down to the lodge with my family on a winter night and look at the lights from the displays and from the thousands of cars. That's the thing we never thought of, the light show put on by the visiting cars. It really is something, and to look down on all of that and know you had something to do with it . . . well, that makes for a very special feeling."

I looked over at Randy Worls after I helped to throw the switch on the Festival of Lights, and he was beaming brighter than anything in the park. He had every reason to.

★ ★

A TREE GROWS IN SOUTHOLD

★ LEWIS EDSON
Southold, New York

If you're like me, you've probably never stopped to think about the people who have lovingly planted and cared for your Christmas tree before you entered the picture. I know that after I've carted the thing home, the only thing I'm thinking about is curling up in front of a nice warm fire with some hot buttered rum and a couple of Santa's little helpers to take care of me. But more than a hundred thousand people in this country do seasonal work in our growing Christmas tree industry, and one of them is a fellow named Lewis Edson, whose Santa's Christmas Tree Farm just opened for business on Long Island's North Fork last season.

"We used to joke around here that I had a name for each and every one of our trees," says Lew of the seventy-five thousand plantings on his forty-acre farm. "They're my babies, and I thought I'd hate to see them go." But go they will, at the rate of about five thousand trees each season, which makes Lew's farm one of the largest "choose and cut" Christmas tree operations in the New York metropolitan area. In fact, it's one of the only such operations a New Yorker is likely to find.

Most Christmas trees are grown on thousand-acre plantations in places like Wisconsin or Minnesota, or in Canada, where real estate is relatively cheap. In the New York market, where land is at a premium, most Christmas trees are imported and sold on vacant lots in the weeks-long season, and the available farmland is put to more lucrative use. That is, until Lew Edson came along.

"The money is not our first priority at this point," Lew says. "The farm had been in our family for years, and when our potato farms were hard hit a few years ago, I thought about doing something different with the land. I wanted to do something that would be fun, almost like a hobby, that wouldn't take all my time and would be a plus for the community." Lew, who runs a successful realty business in Southold, thought briefly of turning the place into a vineyard (the eastern half of Long Island has fast become one of this country's leading wine regions, with over two dozen wineries), but he realized such an investment would take too much of his time. And he thought about subdividing the land for commercial or residential use, before deciding that the last thing the area needed was another condominium community or shopping mall.

So, after considerable research and planning, Lew planted his first seedlings in 1981 and began a meticulous six-year growth cycle that would someday put him in business. Now here's the good part: Lew's first batch of trees came in more than a year ahead of schedule, and he had to race to put up a sign and a storefront to open shop in time for his first season. "Trees are like people, in that you get some that grow faster than others," he explains. "They don't grow like little soldiers, all at the same time." No, I guess they don't.

By 1985, with over seventy thousand trees planted, Lew figured there had to be a tree ready for his personal use. "I took my two tree experts (daughter Channing, eight, and son Evans, fourteen) and told them to pick one out for us," he recalls. (He's got two other kids—Lisa, twenty-one, and Riley, twenty—and his wife, Deborah, looks after the real estate business during the busy Christmas tree season.) "Channing came back to me and said, 'Daddy! There aren't any trees here. They're not big enough.' But I told her that there were seventy thousand trees in the ground, there had to be a few ready to take home." Lew's experts eventually found him three trees—one for the real estate office, one for Grandma, and one for hearth and home—and his family got its first taste of what business as usual would be like around Christmastime in the years to come.

"I can't tell you how wonderful it feels to sit with your family under a Christmas tree you've grown yourself," he says with the glow of a yule log. "After five seasons on your hands and knees in the dirt, digging and cutting and planting and spraying and fertilizing, there is a tremendous sense of pride and satisfaction. In the office I would try to discreetly

lead the customers to the tree and fish for compliments."
These, I suppose, are the fringe benefits of life in the Christmas tree business. I know what he's talking about, though.
I've never grown my own Christmas tree, but I've cut them;
as a kid, that was one of my biggest thrills, trudging out in
the snow, having my way with the tree, and carting it back
inside. I used to sit back, after we'd strung up the lights, and
I'd be as proud as could be.

Lew Edson, forty-five, is a big, almost lumbering kind of
guy, an appropriate description for someone in the tree business. He reminds me a little bit of my old friend Roy Clark,
the country singer and picker. He's got the same build, the
same honest-looking face. At one time Lew was the director
of new site development for McDonald's, a pretty substantial
job for a guy who quit high school at sixteen. And come to
think of it, his real estate offices (he opened his main office
in 1976 and a second one six months later) look a whole lot
like McDonald's storefronts. They sit underneath big, invit-
ing signs, on neatly landscaped property, with plenty of parking for impulse home owners and renters. "That's the
McDonald's philosophy," he acknowledges, "spending the
upfront money to bring in the customers, and that's the same
philosophy I want to bring to the tree farm." Plans are under
way at the farm for the refurbishing of a main house, to be
used as an office and waiting area and storefront, and for the
construction of a matching barn; he is also putting in parking
spaces for more than fifty cars. By the time he sold his first
tree, he had invested more than $250,000 in the operation,
not counting the cost of the land.

Lew says the things most people look for in a Christmas
tree are fragrance, needle size, fullness, and height. He also
says his customers are more knowledgeable about trees in
general than he would have thought. "They come in here
and they know what they want," he says. "They know what
to look for, which means I better know what I'm doing. And
I act like I know exactly what I'm doing."

What he's doing is something, really. "Look," he says,
"there aren't many things a family can do together these
days, but we're hoping we become a family tradition. We're
hoping that every fall people will jump in their cars, come

out and tag a tree, and return to cut it and pick it up in the few weeks before Christmas. It's a wonderful outing for a nice fall afternoon. We have no intention of selling the land, and we tell our customers that we hope someday their children will come back with their children to our farm."

Now here's a guy who can see the forest for the trees.

★ ★

Betsy and Bud Smith's front lawn, Christmas 1974.

THIS IS ACTUALLY SOMEONE'S HOUSE!

★ BUD & BETSY SMITH
Roslyn, Pennsylvania

This story, I'm sad to say, doesn't have a happy ending, and that's a crying shame. But that doesn't mean it shouldn't be told, because oh, what a wonderful story it was! And what a wonderful story it could still be if it weren't for a few bad eggs spoiling the carton.

Bud and Betsy Smith are something of a legend in the Philadelphia area, deservedly so. For twenty-one Christmases they decorated their modest house and three-quarter-acre property in suburban Roslyn, Pennsylvania, with the

AMERICA IS MY NEIGHBORHOOD

most inventive, elaborate, and breathtaking display of lights and moving, life-size characters you're ever likely to see, and for twenty-one Christmases, families would trek from near and far to see what new wonders their magic had wrought.

People who didn't know Bud and Betsy personally knew their house intimately. There was a time when the entire neighborhood would pitch in to help, with local kids returning home early from school to help paint the fantastic displays and local parents helping with the wiring, the costume making, and the heavy lifting. When they talk about those days it just sounds wonderful; people don't go out of their way for each other like that anymore, not even in the neighborhood of my imagination.

Before they dismantled the display each year, Bud and Betsy were already planning their next effort. Each year, from early December to just after New Year's, the Smiths would outdo themselves. "That was the whole point," Bud says, "to make each display better than the last."

By all accounts—and, believe me, it would take an independent accounting firm to keep track of the steady stream of testimonials the Smiths have received over the years—they succeeded. You had to see this display to believe it. Thousands of bright lights, dozens of full-scale animated figurines and moving contraptions bathed the Smiths' house and yard in a happy, festive glow that lit up the whole neighborhood. Everything looked like the work of a professional craftsman, from a giant mechanized caterpillar to a merry-go-round being ridden by four bugs. A friend who built the floats for Gimbel's Thanksgiving Day Parade helped with many of the displays. It was like a Broadway production on somebody's front lawn. The Smiths, with a gracious assist from their friends and neighbors, even dressed up as Christmas and storybook characters for three live-action song and dance shows each evening.

"Every year we had a theme," Bud recalls. "Sometimes it was Disneyland, sometimes it was the Peanuts characters, in 1976 it was the bicentennial, but every year it was a new theme. We didn't want it to just be Christmas and Santa Claus each year, we wanted it to be more than that." But, of course, you can't ignore the man in the big red suit, and for many years Bud and Betsy featured an animated Santa in the window of their home, which communicated with children outside through a closed-circuit television hook-up. A live Santa would give out candy canes to visiting children, and on some nights he'd dispense several thousand.

"If you ever had a party for a couple of hundred people, then you know what it was like," Betsy explains, "except that for us we had that party every night." Strangers, sometimes several hundred at a time, several thousand in a day, would look in from the street, while friends and neighbors gathered inside in a month-long open-house party. "Once in a while it was like they'd never leave," Betsy says, "but we loved it. We wouldn't have done it if we didn't love it. It got so that people knew our house as the 'Christmas House,' and they'd look forward to coming by every year."

People came from all over the map to see this wondrous spectacle. Once, on vacation in Jamaica, Bud was approached by a man who'd seen his incredible display on television. On their travels, when they mentioned their hometown, people would want to know if they'd ever seen the "Christmas House" and be delighted to learn that the Smiths were the proprietors. They were written up in every local newspaper, and their display was covered by camera crews from every local television station. In 1973, when President Nixon asked people to curb their Christmas lights displays on account of the energy crisis, members of the national media called to see if Bud and Betsy would honor the president's request. "We were in a quandary that year," Bud recalls, "so we decided to do a poll to see what the public thought. People called from all over and said they wouldn't light their lights this year so that we could light ours. It was overwhelming." The Smiths took a formal vote over a five-day period and came away with 3,250 in favor of lighting the display and only 47 opposed. I guess that's what you'd call a landslide.

This whole thing started from a childhood promise Bud made to himself. "When I was thirteen or so, my sister took me out to see some Christmas lights," he remembers. "I was enthralled, and I said to myself, 'Boy, that's what I'm gonna do!' So all through the next year I saved my money, every penny, and when Christmas came around again I bought some lights for our house." But wait, that wasn't quite the start of something big. "No, no," Bud continues. "My dad was a bit of a Scrooge, and he told me he didn't want to pay for the additional electric bills, so he made me take them down. I was crushed, but I vowed that one day I'd decorate my own home." In 1961, when he was twenty-eight years old, Bud made good on his words; in their first year in their new house, and their first Christmas as husband and wife, Bud and Betsy launched an annual tradition that would last for most of the next twenty-three years.

Which brings us to the sad part of Bud and Betsy's story. The ghosts of Christmases past put the Smiths out of the good cheer business temporarily for the 1978 holiday season and permanently following the 1983 celebration. "We had a big problem with vandalism," Bud tells. "They were stealing floodlights—I think one night we lost twenty—and some people would take our characters out in the street and smash them." The annual display was costly to begin with (Bud won't tell what his electric bills cost him), but the heartless destruction and theft of his handmade delights made the annual event prohibitively expensive. One year, hand-crafted Fred Flintstone and Mickey Mouse figures were destroyed. Once the Smiths' nativity scene was stolen, and another year it was set on fire. The Smiths' front lawn, and the streets surrounding their home, was littered and trashed.

In 1978, Bud and Betsy called a temporary halt to their annual celebrations, and instead of brightly colored lights and characters, their front lawn featured only a large sign explaining their decision and asking for thoughts on correcting the problem. Their suggestion box was filled to overflowing. People sent money to help defray any costs (Bud and Betsy still have the uncashed checks from many annual visitors). Thousands expressed hope that the situation would improve and that the Smiths would reconsider in time for the next holiday season. "For the few that did damage, we had one hundred thousand who told us they appreciated what we were doing," Bud recalls. "That's what made it all worthwhile." Their dilemma attracted so much attention, we even got wind of it down in Washington.

So they decided to give it another shot. The second time around lasted for another five wonderful seasons, but after the 1983 display, the Smiths decided they'd had enough. "It wasn't just the vandalism," Betsy admits, "although that was the biggest part of it."

"We lost a lot of our helpers as people got older," Bud says with a touch of regret in his voice. "Kids moved out of the neighborhood, and people got other interests. All of a sudden there weren't too many friends around to help, and it can be backbreaking work."

The Smiths developed other interests, too. They've purchased a camper and every weekend drive to a Pennsylvania campground and park themselves in the great outdoors. "We decorate the camper," Betsy says, "and everywhere we go during the holidays we stop traffic."

I bet they do.

But what a sad commentary it is that the tireless devotion of these good people can be spoiled by a handful of hoodlums. The silver lining to all this is that even a couple of bad eggs can't tarnish a cherished memory. Bud and Betsy's warm-hearted efforts will live long in the hearts of those who had the good fortune to share in the joy and wonder of their annual displays.

WITH everything else it's got going for it, Christmas is also a time of homecoming. At NBC, it's a chance to visit with the hardworking people who've been scattered around the globe, as they pass through New York or Washington to spend a few days with their families. At home, it's a chance to tidy up our scattered clan and bring the entire family under one roof, even if it's just for one meal. It's like a magnet, Christmas, drawing friends and loved ones together from parts unknown. For that I'm grateful.

I'm also grateful for the cards and gifts and home-baked goodies that can crowd me out of my office during the holidays. Really, our daily bundle of mail is twice its usual size during December, and it comes in smelling like a wonderful bakery. Mail call was never such a pleasure!

But most of all I'm grateful for the way Christmas makes everyone around us feel. We could all go to school on the way the Christmas spirit has infected the folks you've met in this chapter, folks like them you probably already know in your hometown. They teach us that Christmas is not a time of year; it's a state of mind. And it's a state of mind I don't mind at all.

The pin-up boy of WRC radio.

7 Voices of America

I LOVE RADIO.

For as long as I can remember, I've had a hankering to send this great, big, booming voice of mine out over the airwaves to the huddled masses.

By the time I was eight years old, I was hooked on the medium. That was the year my mother dropped me off at the old Earle Theatre in Washington to see a matinee while she went shopping, a big outing for a wet-behind-the-ears kid like me. Well, the show ended well before my mother's shopping spree, so I ventured out for some exploring. I was always an antsy kid, and on this restless occasion the ants in my pants took me wandering around to one of the office buildings adjacent to the theater; I had my sights set on my very own personal tour of WTOP radio, one of the leading local stations of the day. I guess you could say I was a self-starter (or a restless little brat, take your pick).

Anyway, I got off the elevator at the WTOP floor, and I walked in like I owned the place, peering and prancing around where I shouldn't have. Lucky for me, the station's sweet receptionist had a soft spot in her heart for wet-behind-the-ears kids, and she showed me around. I got the grand tour of the place. She took me back to one of the studios where a live broadcast was going on. What a thrill! I was so quiet you could hear my heart thumping. When the broadcast was through, she even introduced me to the CBS correspondent on duty, a tall, thin, ruddy-faced man named Eric Sevareid.

That was it for me. Eric Sevareid became my inspiration, my radio role model, and I couldn't wait to get home and retreat to our basement to set up a radio station of my own. I couldn't wait to be like Eric Sevareid. I split three yo-yos in half and hammered the halves into the wall to serve as pretend dials on a pretend control panel. I used a soap dish for a microphone, and I was in business.

After a while, what we used to call "pretend" radio wasn't good enough. A bunch of the neighborhood kids got together to form a radio club, and we gradually turned my basement into a real radio station with a small phono oscillator. With a microphone and a miniature transmitter, we could play and announce records to radios within a hundred yards or so of our studio, which basically meant that good old Mr. Vance next door could listen to our makeshift doings (and he often did). It wasn't much, but it was something.

We took as our name the call letters WSSD, which stood for yours truly, and two of my friends, named Sharp and Derek. We also had my good friends Jimmy Rudin and Roger Gordon, whose names for some reason didn't quite fit. We had our own newscasts and commentary, and we even sold advertising; if you owned the local drugstore or grocery store, and you wanted to get a sales pitch to Mr. Vance, ours was the only game in town. At a rate of twenty-five cents a commercial, you might say we were the most cost-efficient buy in broadcasting. (Roger soon outgrew WSSD, and he bought a high-powered phono oscillator of his own, this one with a broadcast range of five miles, except he got himself into a little bit of trouble with the FCC when his broadcasts interfered with Pan Am's communications channel at nearby National Airport. The sky was truly the limit in our radio club.)

A few years later, Roger and I muscled our way onto WOL —an honest-to-goodness, nothing-pretend-about-it radio station in the D.C. area—with a show called "High School Hit Parade," a weekly top-ten-countdown show of our own devising, complete with chatter and contests and prizes. Even though I was still only in high school myself, I was beginning to think I could make a living from my childhood obsession. Around this time I had also hooked up with a small FM station in the area called WCFM, and I was the announcer for their weekly high school news program on Saturday nights; in those days, most radios couldn't receive the FM signal, and I remember my parents had to go to a neighbor's house to listen to the broadcast.

Yet I was already looking ahead to my next step. I'd had my eyes and heart set on a job as a page at WRC, the local NBC radio station. I counted the days until my sixteenth birthday, and then I went down to the station for an interview. Memory tells me that I wowed the heck out of these people, although a second opinion would likely tell you that wasn't quite the truth. They probably had some heck left after they were through with the likes of me. In any event, there wasn't an opening to be had (or so they said), so I made a pest of myself every week until they offered me a one-shot deal as a substitute page. If things worked out, there was the chance I could be a regular substitute. Again, it wasn't much, but it was something. My first day on the job was Saturday, September 16, 1950. I was petrified. I remember going over to Epiphany Episcopal Church on G Street, to put in a good word for myself. I wanted so badly to do well that I thought I'd need some big help.

Turns out I did okay, because a week later I was made a regular weekend substitute, eventually moving into a permanent weekend slot. The job itself wasn't much—getting coffee and manning the station's switchboards—but I couldn't have been happier. I had my own uniform, with the old NBC emblem of a fire coming out of a microphone, and I would regularly cross paths with the likes of Elizabeth Taylor, Spencer Tracy, Roy Rogers, and Dale Evans. (Once I disappeared with Eleanor Roosevelt's coat, and she had to borrow somebody else's to leave the building; I thought I'd never live that one down.) But most of all, I was a part of the most exciting business I could imagine. I was on my way.

A lot of folks in this business have been bitten by the same bug that took a bite out of an antsy eight-year-old kid named Willard Scott. Nobody in broadcasting has a more intimate relationship with his or her audience than a traditional radio personality—really, there's no match for the years-long give and take of the airwaves—and next you'll meet some of the best and brightest on-air personalities the medium has ever known. Together they embody the true spirit of broadcasting, and they serve as a link to days gone by, when radio played a much deeper role in all our lives.

Here goes.

* *

THE OTHER JOY BOY

★ **ED WALKER**
Bethesda, Maryland

Ed Walker is like a brother to me. He's been a partner and a friend for close to thirty-five years, and he continues to be a trailblazing force in radio in the Washington, D.C., area. Eddie is quick on his feet when he's on the air; really, he's got one of the sharpest minds I've ever come across. He's also got this rich, resonant voice, perfectly suited to the medium, and he's got the uncanny knack of making his listeners feel like long-lost friends, almost like one of the family. The grabber for this one, though, is that Eddie Walker is blind,

Putting ourselves to sleep, me and "Joy Boy" Ed Walker.

but you'd never know it to hear him work, unless of course he's joking about it.

We first met when I entered American University in the fall of 1951; Eddie was a year ahead of me, and he had already started up a little campus radio station called WAMU. (WAMU, by the by, still exists and is one of the most successful college-based radio stations in the country.) Anyhow, Eddie and I were introduced by a mutual friend (Roger Gordon, again, from my basement radio days), and for one reason or another we just clicked. It was instantaneous. Actually, our introduction was sort of one-sided. I was a bit of a sneak in those days, and I just plopped myself down next to Eddie, ever so quietly, while he was on the air. Yeah, yeah, it was a lousy thing to do, I know, but I'm glad I did it. It got our relationship off to a fast start.

Eddie was so absorbed in doing his show that I thought he didn't hear me come in—at least that's what I'd hoped—so I waited for an opening in his monologue before I started running my mouth off. I thought I'd startle him, trip him up a step or two, but he never missed a beat. We traded quips back and forth as if we'd known each other for years. We just fell right into it. Our immediate rapport was like something developed and polished over a period of several years. We were on the same wavelength. We had the same sense of humor, the same love of people, the same passion for the medium. We worked together, in some form or another, for the next twenty-five years, and we'll be close for the rest of our lives.

The two of us are probably best remembered for our long-running stint as "The Joy Boys" of WRC radio, the NBC affiliate down in Washington, but that's not the only thing we did together. We started out professionally on a show called "Going AWOL," which aired on WOL-AM at eleven P.M. to midnight on Sundays. Nobody, and I mean nobody, was listening to the radio at that hour, except of course our immediate families. They had to listen to us. But we must have been doing something right, because soon we'd landed a record show, and "Going AWOL" was expanded to Saturday nights, when literally tens of folks we didn't know tuned us in. We were moving up in the world of big-time radio.

Eventually we moved our act over to WRC, with a show called "Two at One" (Eddie was always great with titles), and he took over my afternoon radio show during my Navy days. The folks at WRC tried us out at every conceivable time slot, day or night, until we landed for a long spell at the evening drive time slot in 1963.

As "The Joy Boys," the two of us finally became the local institutions we had always thought we richly deserved to be, doing zany skits and bits and tomfooling our way into the hearts of the greater Washington area. Our theme song, "We Are the Joy Boys of Radio," sung to the tune of the old "Billboard March" you've all heard at the circus, fast became a popular ditty on the tips of local tongues. We were even given a backhanded tribute in the movie *Ensign Pulver*, when a soused Burl Ives, properly anesthetized for a ship-board appendix operation, lapsed into a drunken rendition of our trademark song. And we were daily given a full-fledged, forehanded compliment by the WRC staff members, who would sit in the studio on their lunch hours and listen to our antics. "That was something," Eddie remembers. "I mean, for those folks to give up their lunch hour to listen to us, that really says something about the work we were doing."

Like most people I know who are fascinated by radio, the young Ed Walker suffered from the same imaginings I did as a child. "The legend in my family is that the first complete sentence I ever spoke was, 'Turn on the radio,' " he jokes. "My mother would always swear it's true." Like me, Eddie also jury-rigged a "pretend" radio station in his basement. "By the time I was twelve or thirteen, I had an oscillator set up to where I could broadcast for several feet," he says. "For me, the radio took the place of the funnies, the comics, even of some books. Because I couldn't read the things the other kids were reading, my fantasy world was the radio."

Not long after I left Washington for the "Today" show, Eddie landed a wonderful assignment with a morning television show called "A.M. Washington," on what was then WMAL-TV. I was thrilled when I learned he'd gotten the job, thrilled not only for Eddie, but for the fact that there was a program director somewhere in this business big and bold enough to put a blind man in front of the cameras. I mean, not being able to see is not as much of a handicap for a radio personality as it is for a television star, and there was some question whether television audiences would accept a blind man as the host of a morning talk show.

But Eddie, God bless him, managed to pull the thing off for five years, all the time without much in the way of incident or fanfare. "It wasn't a very mobile show," he recalls. "I kept us pretty much tied to the set. But there was one time, I remember, when we got a little adventurous. We had some gal from the Washington Zoo on with a baby tiger. I was supposed to feed him milk out of a bottle, and everything was fine until I heard this baby tiger come up sucking air. I don't know, I guess I'd dropped the bottle, and all of a sudden I felt something at my shoes. I thought sure I was gonna be minus one foot by the time we got the tiger out of there."

Yet despite his successful tenure on the tube (he never did lose his foot to that tiger, incidentally), radio remains first in Eddie's heart, in his blood. He still hosts his own radio program in Washington, and he does double duty on a National Public Radio program focusing on the achievements of handicapped individuals. "It's much more personal," he says of radio. "I'll always stay involved in it in some form or another. In television there are too many people involved, so in a way it's easier because there are so many people to do your work for you. But in radio you've got your hands in everything. I grew up with radio. You know, like they say, radio is theater of the mind. It leaves something to the imagination."

In a medium that leaves something to the imagination, Ed Walker has left almost nothing to the imagination. He's done it all—as a disc jockey, talk personality, announcer, and co-median—and he continues to do it all. "A television director I know once said to me I've landed in the best-possible field," Eddie told me recently. "And you know, he's right. I'm getting paid for doing what I enjoy, something I'd prob-ably do anyway if somebody gave me the chance. And here I am making a career out of it."

But it's not just any career Ed Walker is making out of it. He's overcome what to many would seem great obstacles to make for himself one of the standout careers in the broad-casting business. I am proud to have worked with him, prouder still to call him a friend.

★ ★

WHY IS THIS MAN SMILING?

★ GARY OWENS
Encino, California

Gary Owens is a model announcer. In fact, every time you hear someone lampoon the old-time radio announcers, there's a good chance the parody is modeled after Gary's rich and flamboyant style and his full-bodied voice. Gary himself contributed to his now stereotypical image for years as the forked-tongue-in-cheek announcer on the old Rowan and Martin's "Laugh-In" shows. You remember, the guy with the checkered suits whose hand was forever cupped around his ear in the style of the forties broadcasters? Yup, that was Gary.

You might say Gary Owens does Gary Owens better than anybody. He's got his voice down pat. I guess when you're born with a set of boffo vocal cords like Gary's, you can't help but land in radio for a living. As an announcer, I've been

*What a set of vocal cords! Here's Gary
Owens in classic radio announcer
pose.*

a fan of his for years—he's one of the busiest voice-over men
in the business (he did 1,200 commercials last year alone!),
and he has more fun doing what he's doing than should be
legally allowed—but I didn't get to work with him until recently. Gary served as my announcer/second banana on a
pilot I did for a television talk show. The pilot was produced
by Columbia Pictures Television, under the brilliantly con-
ceived title of "The Willard Scott Show" (they paid somebody a lot of money to come up with that one), and I can't
tell you how delighted I was when I learned we'd signed
Gary to do the announcing chores.

Of course, Gary wasn't exactly out looking for a job. He
already had something like five or six other pilots in his
professional pipeline, including a revival of that talent show
of the absurd, "The Gong Show." (A note to you trivia buffs:
When that show was first syndicated, Gary served as its original host, before the inimitable Chuck Barris stepped in to
make a fool of himself and of his guests.) On top of all that,
he hosts his own radio show in Los Angeles and a syndicated
radio show of rock 'n' roll oldies, which reaches some four
hundred stations around the country. Not bad for a kid from
South Dakota. Not bad at all.

Actually, Gary's broadcasting career is akin to mine in
more ways than you might think. We both grew up in a small-

town environment with an inexplicable passion for radio, and we both worked our way up through the medium's rank and file to enjoy some measure of success. "I remember we didn't have television the same time as the rest of the country," Gary recalls, "which means radio was a part of our lives for a lot longer than it would have been if I'd lived someplace else. I loved radio as a kid, and I still do. I used to broadcast my own show, on my own station, with an oscillator from my bedroom. I'd send out the signal to about a two-block radius from my room." Gary's makeshift radio station went by the call letters of KGAR, borrowing the first three letters of his first name, probably on the advice of that same guy who came up with the name for my talk show pilot.

His first real radio job came when he was still in high school, at a tiny 250-watt radio station in Mitchell, South Dakota, called KORN-AM (no kidding). There, Gary hosted something called "The KORN Palace City," for the princely sum of $75 per week. (I always love hearing about someone's first job in radio, because it reminds me of the way things used to be.) After stops in Omaha, Denver, and San Francisco, Gary graduated to the big time in Los Angeles, where he has held a regularly scheduled spot in the hearts of local listeners for the past twenty-five years.

"Radio has been terrific to me," Gary admits. "It's always been the key, the foundation for whatever career I've managed to build. Television, too, in a way, but that's been as an outgrowth of radio. Actually, what I really wanted to be was a cartoonist. That was my true dream, and in a way it still is. But I got sidetracked by my voice. Announcing has always come easy to me, I was always the emcee at shows in high school and college."

What does he make of all the attention heaped on his singularly wonderful voice? "I'm flattered when people tell me what an unusual voice I have," he admits, "but my voice is pretty much of a put-on. There's a lot of false bravado in my voice. If you'll notice, a lot of times it sounds like I'm saying something terrifically important when in fact it's meaningless. That's one of the reasons we were so successful with my character on 'Laugh-In.' You know, on the one hand I'd sound so serious, but what I was saying was some nonsense like 'The Mystery Earlobe'!" (He sends his deep voice even deeper for this last part.)

Put-on or otherwise, Gary's deep voice is everywhere. I know I can't turn the dial, any dial, without hearing it. You probably hear him half a dozen times a day without even realizing it—on commercials, cartoons (he's provided the voice for more than 1,400 animated characters, including two of my favorites, Space Ghost and Roger Ramjet), network promos, you name it. And if you're like me, you probably can't sit and talk to Gary without cracking a smile. You know this voice! You love this voice! Talking to Gary is like talking to Hollywood. Even on a simple telephone call, he sounds like he's wearing a tuxedo.

Gary has turned on his voice, and on his Hollywood base, to help win enough acting roles to make a fledgling actor foam at the mouth. I must confess, he makes me jealous with all the work he's done in front of the cameras. He's appeared in countless television shows, including "McHale's Navy," "The Green Hornet," "Captain Nice" (starring "St. Elsewhere"'s William Daniels) and "The Munsters" (he played one of Herman Munster's neighbors in a recurring role), and in dozens of movies from every major Hollywood studio. All of this, in combination with his long-running role on "Laugh-In" (Gary, Ruth Buzzi, Arte Johnson, and Messrs. Rowan and Martin were the only folks to appear on the show for its duration), has helped to make Gary a household face as well as a household voice.

"My voice has taken me pretty far," Gary reasons, "but I don't think that's the only reason I'll always work in radio. That might have been what brought me to the medium, but it's not what keeps me there. Radio is unlike any other form of entertainment or communication we have. It's spontaneous, it's live, and it's unpredictable. You don't have all this postproduction stuff you have to worry about in television. You don't have to get dressed up. It's all theater of the mind in radio. Everything is left to the imagination. In radio, anything is possible."

Don't I know it.

★ ★

*One of radio's Golden Oldies, Ed
Herlihy.*

RADIO DAYS

★ ED HERLIHY
New York, New York

Now here's another one for you trivia buffs: Ed Herlihy, the man who for nineteen years hosted the "Horn & Hardart Children's Hour" on radio and television, and the man who has lent his announcing voice to countless NBC programs for over fifty years, could have been Ed McMahon. Well, sort of. Were it not for a years-ago glitch in the NBC scheduling, Ed Herlihy could have been sitting on "The Tonight Show" couch for the past twenty-five years, trading quips and guffaws with the top names in the entertainment business, and he could be smiling on the face of millions of junk-mail sweepstakes envelopes from coast to coast.

"That's fate for you," says Ed (Herlihy, not McMahon), who served as "The Tonight Show" announcer and sidekick during a twenty-six-week period in 1962, between the hosting reigns of Jack Paar and Johnny Carson. "They were filling in with everybody," Ed remembers. "It was like a revolving door of celebrity guest hosts." The revolving door was spun, usually for one week at a time, by people like Soupy Sales, Groucho Marx, Jerry Lewis, and—get this, Joan Rivers!—Arlene Francis, the first woman to host the program. Skitch Henderson led "The Tonight Show" band during this period and stayed on for the first four years of Carson's tenure.

"They asked me to do the show permanently while I was still doing 'Kraft Television Theater,' " Ed remembers. "I was able to do it only because we juggled the schedule one night each week." ("The Tonight Show" was taped weeknights between seven-thirty and nine in those days, except for one night each week when it was bumped to eight-thirty to ten to accommodate Ed's schedule.) "Then when they brought Johnny Carson in, they offered me the job but told me I'd have to give up the Kraft job, and I thought, Well, this is a new show, and 'Kraft Television Theater' has been around a long time. Maybe I shouldn't chance it. Well, you know the rest of that story."

But the story, thankfully, doesn't end there for Ed Herlihy. It doesn't even begin there, although his would-be imprint on "The Tonight Show" serves nicely as an introduction to our visit. To my mind, Ed Herlihy has had one of the most remarkable announcing careers in the short history of the broadcasting business. What I wouldn't give for the chance to have seen and done half the things he has! Think about it: he announced his first NBC radio broadcast in 1936, and he lived and worked and prospered through the early glory days of the medium.

Oh, what a time that must have been, and Ed Herlihy was there, front and center, for all of it. (Once again, I'm jealous.) He was there in black tie and tails, announcing for Sigmund Romberg and the NBC Orchestra, to a live audience of over 1,500, in the studio where they now tape "Saturday Night Live." ("I always loved to dance," he recalls of the days when live music filled our airwaves, "and when the orchestra would play I would be waltzing off in the corner with one of the singers.") He had his thick and friendly voice right smack in the middle of our first game show broadcasts ("Honeymoon in New York"), our first soap operas ("Against the Storm," "Vic 'n Sade," and "Just Plain Bill"), and our first variety shows ("The Kraft Music Hall" and "Hildegarde's The Raleigh Room"). He's seen it all in this business, and he's provided the voice-over and commentary to most of it.

"I'm the last of the old farts," says Ed with his characteristic chuckle and self-deprecating charm and wit. "I'm probably one of the few guys still around from the days when we did those on-the-spot, special-events broadcasts." Ed remembers one such broadcast, when he was the junior hand on an announce team sent to Roosevelt Field on Long Island to cover Howard Hughes's return from his round-the-world trip.

"I was the new kid, so they had me stationed at the very end of the airfield," Ed says. "He wasn't supposed to get as far as me without one of our other reporters getting to him first. But sure enough, they weren't able to get to him, and he was coming my way, and I jumped out onto the tarmac and pulled off one of the greatest ad-libs of my life. My mike was live, and I said something like 'Wait here a minute, I'm going to get Mr. Hughes,' something brilliant like that, and I just left my mike and disappeared into the crowd. We were live, and for all I know we broadcast dead air for the next few minutes while I went begging and pleading for an interview." Stuff like that doesn't happen anymore, unfortunately; I miss the days when things were shoestring enough to allow for an occasional mix-up, and I know Ed misses them, too. I think when things went wrong—and oh, did they sometimes go wrong!—we were able to seem more human to our listeners, like the times we'd flub our lines in the middle of a bit or when we'd botch the ad copy to the point of ridiculousness. Today, everything is mapped and orchestrated to the nth degree. There's no room for error, and that's a shame: to err is human, some bard once said, but to err on radio is simply divine.

Ed differs from other old radio hands like Gary Owens, Ed Walker, and myself in that he never really aspired to the medium. "I always thought of myself as an actor," he says, "and I still do. But I was intrigued by it, enough to pursue it as a career. My godmother used to tell me I should find work in this nice radio thing everybody's talking about because I had such a nice voice."

So Ed took his nice voice to WLOE, a one-hundred-watt radio station in Boston, where he hawked his wares for $10 per week. (Ten dollars! Can you believe it?) From there he moved to WORC in nearby Worcester, Massachusetts, and a raise to $25 per week. (There, now we're talking!) "I remember I spent nine dollars on room and board, sent ten dollars home, and had a hell of a time with the rest," he says. "We still had the old carbon microphones back in those days." He then returned to Boston with stints at WHDH and WEEI. By the time he reached the big time, as an NBC announcer based in New York, Ed was earning a healthy salary of $198.50 each month.

"Those were the halcyon days of radio," Ed says, looking back. "None of us had any idea of what we had, where we were going, what we were doing. Not really. I miss those days now, I really do. Today everything is planned and plotted and test-marketed. Then we just went on the air with what we had, and we were able to be innocent in a way that's no longer possible. Those were some times."

They were some times, and a look at Ed's credits during that period puts him right on top of any listing of who was who in radio and gives readers today a not-so-subtle clue about what was what in the early days of the medium; he hosted a number of memorable radio programs, including "The Martin and Lewis Show," "The Henny Youngman Show," "Truth or Consequences," "Dick Tracy," "The Falcon," "The Chesterfield Supper Club," "The Horn & Hardart Children's Hour" (which helped, by the by, to launch the careers of Bernadette Peters, Ken Howard, Gregory Hines, and others), "The Kraft Music Hall," and "The Big Show," with Tallulah Bankhead.

"That was pretty much radio's last hurrah," Ed remembers of "The Big Show," which he hosted for NBC in 1949–50. "We didn't know it at the time, but that was really the end of the big live radio broadcasts."

But the end of live radio didn't spell the end of Ed Herlihy's career. Not by any means. Along the way he managed to carve successful careers as a journalist, reporting the news for Universal's "International Newsreel" for over twenty-five years, and as an actor, appearing on Broadway in *Mame,* and in movies like *The Chosen, Zelig,* and *The King of Comedy.* He has also toured extensively in regional productions of *Room Service* (with Eddie Albert), *Damn Yankees* (with Vincent Price), *Mame* (with Angela Lansbury), and *Showboat* (with Margaret Hamilton) and can currently be seen (or, rather, heard) on Broadway with an off-stage voice-over role in Neil Simon's *Broadway Bound.*

Elected to the Broadcaster's Hall of Fame in 1980, Ed has been lucky to watch an industry grow before his very eyes, and we've been lucky to have him on hand to walk us through the process. "I've seen the whole thing from a very unique vantage point," he says. "We were all pioneers, in a sense, both in radio and in television, and at each step we took the only trail we knew how to take. We had to get from there to here in one way or another, and I don't know if we took the right trails at every turn, but we did get here."

Indeed.

★ ★

"CAN WE TALK?"

★ ANNE KEEFE
St. Louis, Missouri

For my money, Anne Keefe has one of the best jobs in the broadcasting business. As host of an afternoon talk and call-in program on the CBS-owned St. Louis station KMOX-AM, the largest radio station in the country, Anne can put her fingertips on any story at any time. And, as a result, her fingertips often rest squarely on the pulse of the nation's heartland.

"St. Louis is kind of an egghead town," says Anne, who has hosted her KMOX program for over ten years, "and by that I mean there are no real blue-collar industries here. Our big companies are Kodak and Bausch and Lomb and Xerox, so a lot of our listeners are engineers, educated people,

"The city is my classroom."—Anne Keefe.

professional people. As a result we're able to do a smart show, we're able to play 'up' to our audience, and we're able to attract the best-possible guests. KMOX is a way of life with the people here. This is middle America, this is where people live."

If something smells rotten in our nation's capital, Anne can pick up the phone and persuade a key Washington player to appear on her program to explain the stench. When Wall Street rocks with yet another investment scandal, she can reach one of the alleged culprits like nobody's business. And when an electrifying new personality hits the entertainment scene like a ton of bricks, you can be sure they'll throw some of their weight in Anne Keefe's direction. (Even a heavy-weight like yours truly appears on Anne's show from time to time.)

"People used to like to listen to one guest for an hour," Anne says, "but that's changed. For some reason they don't have the attention span anymore, so I'm looking to guests for short times. People want a fast-paced *USA Today, People* magazine kind of news, they like their news quick and dirty, and they don't call in anymore to ask questions as much as they call in to give their opinions. They call in and say, 'This is what I think about such-and-such,' and that's that, and because of that I rarely book a guest for the whole hour, people just don't have the patience. Besides, it's a lot easier to get a Senator Proxmire or a Senator Dole for a ten- or fifteen-minute segment than it is to get them to come on for an hour. So I take advantage of that. We've worked the format of the show around to where we can discuss every major issue of the day, with expert commentary from those directly involved in the issues."

More than any other broadcaster I know, Anne Keefe has a true dialogue with her listeners, with her community. The local ratings show that she reaches 150,000 listeners each quarter hour, a staggering number that doesn't begin to account for those she can reach in parts unknown around the country (the KMOX fifty-thousand-watt clear-channel signal reaches thirty-five states during Anne's time slot, more during the evening hours). "If I'm talking about the governor, you know, about some new policy or another, then there's a good chance he'll call me during the show to put his two cents in," Anne says. "We'll put him on the air and let him have his say, because, after all, my show is a dialogue. It's his show as much as it is mine. He's even called from his car phone a couple of times."

Anne Keefe has got this wonderful deep voice—a raspy-throated drawl she attributes to years of junk food and cigarettes and Irish whiskey—and a delightful, questioning personality, two qualities that combine to make her one of the most distinctive personalities in local radio. "What you hear is the result of years of abuse," she jokes, and although she is referring to her voice, you get the sense she also means her other qualities as an interviewer.

Actually, Anne says she doesn't think of herself so much as an interviewer as she does as a teacher. "That's my true role," she admits. "I'm here to move a story along, to help people understand the things which affect their lives, to ask questions the average listener doesn't have a chance to ask. I do my homework before a guest appears, the same way a teacher would prepare a lesson plan, but then I have to make sure the class is interesting. The city is my classroom." (Some smart KMOX promotion director should hop on this last as an ad line, pronto.)

Anne got her start in broadcasting up in Rochester, New York, at radio station WHAM, another clear-channel fifty-thousand-watt station. There she worked with her husband on a program called *Hometowners*, a domestic chatter show filled with household hints and family recipes and interviews over country dinners. (God, I miss shows like that!) After only a year on that program, Anne left her freshly planted radio roots behind for a career at the city's sister television station, where she hosted everything from "Romper Room" to a matinee movie call-in program to a local cooking show. She also hosted a hard-news interview program, which led to a spot as a newsroom reporter and weekly anchor for the station's newscasts at six and eleven P.M.

"Basically, I was able to maneuver my schedule at the station around my kids," says Anne, who was divorced in 1962, well before any industry came around to face the problems of single working mothers. "I mean, I had six small kids, and I had to juggle a family and a job. I talk to young women all the time about careers, and I always tell them I don't have a career. I have a job. I happen to like what I do, and I happen to be reasonably well paid for what I do, and I happen to be well known in my community for what I do, but it's not the most important thing in my life. I'm a mother, first and foremost, and when my kids were growing up that always came first. I'm not a broadcast groupie, you know, someone who sat around as a kid using a hairbrush as a microphone. This is a job to me."

When Anne's older children hit their teenage years, she told her station manager she could no longer work the eleven P.M. newscast. Here's someone who really had her priorities straight; I sometimes wonder if I was around enough for my girls, the way Anne made sure she was around for her kids. Of course, Anne was a single parent for much of the time her kids were growing up, so it's a different situation, but she seems to have known exactly what she wanted from motherhood and from broadcasting. "I told the station I had to be home at night," she recalls. "I mean, I couldn't not be there for them, I couldn't not know where they were or what they doing. So I suggested that the station do a noon newscast, which very few stations were doing at the time, and I switched my schedule around so I could work on that. I was able to provide for my family and still be at home for them in the evening. That's the way it's been with most of my job decisions. Things just seem to come along at the right time. I've sort of bumbled my way through life and through what some people call my career, and I've been lucky, which I guess is God's compensation to me for giving me a big nose and a big derriere."

Originally Anne started out in this thing as an actress, but she gave up on her dream after a brief try at show business. "I didn't want to be living in a cold-water flat," she jokes now, "drinking cheap wine and talking about what a great actress I could have been." But acting remained in her blood, and after she established herself with her successful efforts in radio and television, she would scoop up her kids and audition, en masse, for parts in community theater productions of plays like The King and I. (What a wonderful family activity!)

After an AFTRA strike in Rochester in 1976, Anne decided to leave the station, and she struck out for St. Louis in search of a behind-the-camera position in television news. "I was fifty years old, and I still had two kids in college and one in high school," she recalls. "I needed a job, and I thought, Who would hire an old broad like me to read the news?" Well, somebody at KMOX had the good sense to hire an old broad like Anne Keefe (she was the first woman to host a program on that station, actually the only woman until quite recently), and ever since, her listeners in St. Louis and surrounding parts have been in for a treat.

"This is middle America," Anne says of the marketplace she serves. "And when you're out there talking to these people every day, you really get a sense of what they're thinking, what they're feeling. You really feel plugged in. We can talk on the air about things like taxes, but it doesn't hit home for most people until I take a call from someone who tells how the new tax laws will be affecting them. People want to know what their neighbors think, how their neighbors are coping. That's what we're here for. It's like I said, KMOX is a way of life around here, and believe me, we hear from them. Sometimes I'm surprised by people's opinions, sometimes I'm not, but always I'm delighted to hear what the listeners have to say. We wouldn't have a show if it weren't for them."

No, I guess they wouldn't. But then, KMOX wouldn't have the afternoon audience it does if they didn't have Anne Keefe.

I SIT here writing this, and I must confess I'm a bit envious of Anne Keefe's direct pipeline to her audience. Really, she can interact with her listeners in a way I'll never be able to communicate with my viewers. National television, particularly national morning news television, doesn't allow for the informal exchange of ideas you can find on some of our better local radio programs. I look at Anne Keefe, and Gary Owens, and Eddie Walker, and I'm busting at the seams. Boy, would I love another taste of that kind of radio! I used to have something like what they all have now when I did "The Joy Boys" with Eddie in Washington, and I suppose the dialogue and warmth generated by my personal appearances and remote broadcasts get close to what they have with their audiences, but it's not the same. I get letters (you better believe I get letters!), but again, it's not the same.

Ed Herlihy is another story entirely. A radio junkie like myself would love to trade places with him, to have lived and worked through the grand old days of the medium. He tells me stories about live NBC broadcasts, in front of studio audiences of a thousand or more, and I get chills up my spine. (No, there's not a draft in the room as I write, it's just that this sort of thing really gets me going.) The little kid who built a pretend radio station in his basement was dreaming about Ed Herlihy's job! That little kid's gotten a bit bigger over the past few years (okay, he's gotten a lot bigger), but he's still dreaming about Ed Herlihy's job. Go figure.

Radio's been "bery, bery good" to me, as they used to say

on "Saturday Night Live," but it's also been "bery, bery good" to the four veterans you've met here. They've made a lasting contribution to the industry, and they've made a difference in the lives of the people who tune them in. We're lucky to have them in these pages, to be sure, and we're more than lucky to have them behind the microphones.

I may be afraid of bridges, but I'll try anything once, even hot-air ballooning.

8 Fear Strikes Out

I AM A PHOBIC PERSON.

I am prone to palpitations, hyperventilation, and cold sweats, under the right (or, I should say, wrong) circumstances. Put me in an anxious situation, any anxious situation, and I'll white-knuckle my way through it along with the best of them.

What is a phobia? Good question. According to the Phobia Society of America, where I now serve on the board of directors, a phobia is "a severe anxiety reaction to a situation, animal, or object that poses no real threat to life or safety and that doesn't produce fear in nonphobic people." To me that's just a fancy way of saying the fears phobics suffer from are very real, even though they may be afraid of a situation that puts them in no real physical danger.

In my case, the first culprit was a bridge. Specifically, it was the Charleston Bridge, down in Charleston, South Carolina. In 1962, I was puttering around in my Corvair convertible, out for a nice, pleasant drive, when suddenly I was gripped by an overwhelming panic as I approached the Charleston. Nothing like that had ever happened to me, and I had used that bridge regularly, sometimes several times a week. All of a sudden I was dizzy, sweating, and my heart was pumping far faster than it should have been. I had no idea what was coming over me. You can't imagine the horrors that raced through my head, what with my active imagination and all. In those days, you have to remember, phobias were not commonly discussed; there was not a system of support in place the way there is today, and not much was known about effective treatment. Mary was with me on that first day, and together we made our way, slowly, across the bridge. But what I wanted desperately to do was turn around and go home; so much for big, bad Willard staring down the enemy. I crossed that bridge that first time, but only because I had Mary with me. I returned home at the end of that long day determined to beat this thing.

The next Saturday, and every weekend for the next few months, I went out and challenged the Chesapeake Bay Bridge, which was much closer to home. There I was, week in and week out, armed with a six-pack of beer on the front seat alongside me, steeled against the vast expanse of what should have been a harmless crossing. Lest I alarm any of you who are justly worried about the dangers of drinking and driving, the beer was there mostly for emotional support, not for imbibing. (Oh, I sucked those babies back, believe me, but I waited until I was safely home for that.) Anyway, I fought my way across that bridge, back and forth, until the fear subsided. I still get shaken whenever I approach a large bridge, but as James Bond might say, I'm shaken and not stirred. I can handle it.

Today's culprit is my job. Specifically, the hot lights, the attention, and the pressures of live television. Public speaking, which has been my bread and butter between "Today" shows, even gets to me. When I least expect it, my breathing will accelerate, I'll perspire like a professional wrestler or a towel boy in a steam room, and I'll lapse into what is known as a "panic attack." I'm able to control the attacks now, to some degree, through medication and therapy and certain kinds of breathing exercises, but when they first began to occur I wasn't so confident that I'd be able to suffer through them. I used to think I was having a heart attack, when really I was in no physical danger.

Sometimes I'd be backstage before a speech, or off camera before a "Today" show segment, and I'd worry that I couldn't go on. But the show must go on, and so I did, panic attacks and all. People look at me, at the work I do, and they're always surprised to hear of the private anguish I sometimes go through. You wouldn't know it to look at me, but that's part of my job. You wouldn't know it to look at a lot of phobic people, and you'll find them in every field, at every level, in all walks of life.

In between the bridges and my job there have been other culprits, large and small, which I have met and sometimes mastered with varying degrees of success. But because of the public nature of who I am and what I do for a living, I'm less inclined to submit to some of the methods of treatment that have helped many people. One time I went to a therapist who suggested I put a paper bag over my head during an attack. Now, this treatment sometimes makes sense—it's supposed to help regulate your breathing, block out external impulses, and control hyperventilation—although in my case it made no sense at all. I'm sure the good folks at NBC would love me all the way to the poorhouse if I turned up to do the weather looking like some police informant seeking anonymity. (They could bill me as the Unknown Weatherman!) Needless to say, I took my phobic business elsewhere.

I mention that story not only because it's funny (some folks would even suggest that a paper bag over my head would be an improvement), but to demonstrate that all sorts of treatments are available to phobics suffering from all sorts of phobias. I'd like to end the preamble to this chapter with a hopeful message to other phobics like myself: You are not alone. Recent research by the National Institute of Mental Health reports that phobias and related anxiety disorders affect over thirteen million people in this country. I would guess the actual number is four times greater than that. Phobic people have come out of the closet, so to speak, over the last decade or so, but my hunch is that the majority still suffer in private. I've heard from many of you, through my work with the Phobia Society of America and through occasional mentions of my own phobias on the air and on the lecture circuit. I know you're out there, and you are not alone. Take heart. Chances are there's a support group in your area to help you work through your fears. Seek them out.

Read on, and I'll introduce you to three phobic people who escaped their private anguish, sought treatment, and changed their lives in the process.

★ ★

BACK FROM WIT'S END

★ JERILYN ROSS
Washington, D.C.

When she was twenty-five, Jerilyn Ross first felt the fears that would haunt her through most of her young adulthood—a fear of heights and of her own impulses—fears that would soon conspire to lead her to a successful new career. She was in Europe with a friend on a picturesque mountaintop, when suddenly she couldn't rely on herself or trust her own good sense for her safety.

"It was like there was a magnet pulling me to the edge of a cliff, and I was going to jump," she says now from the safe perspective offered by years of living with and through her

"People with panic disorders need not feel alone."—Jerilyn Ross (center) at a Phobia Society conference.

fears and helping others do the same. "It was the most frightening, terrifying feeling I'd ever experienced in my life. The only way I can describe it is that it was like I was hanging on a tightrope by my pinky. I remember feeling like I couldn't control myself." I know the feeling she describes all too well, and I know how frightening it can be.

But the wonderful thing about Jerilyn Ross, now a pretty, brave, and delightful pioneer in the treatment of phobic people, is that she did control herself, and it is her tremendous inner strength and continued control that have helped her to help thousands of others with similar fears and anxieties. Since her first encounter on that mountaintop, Jerilyn has gone on to become the president of the Phobia Society of America, an organization founded in 1980 to serve as a national clearing house for information on panic disorders and phobias and a support group for those who suffer from same. She is also the associate director of the Roundhouse Square Psychiatric Center in Alexandria, Virginia, where she oversees the ongoing therapy of phobic patients. She is one of the most public spokespersons on behalf of phobics and phobia treatments, and she is a living, breathing personification of the most successful type of therapy for phobics—the use of former or current phobics in the treatment process. Hers is a triumphant success story both as a patient and as a therapist.

"It really made me feel like I was crazy," Jerilyn says of the near crippling fear of heights first manifested on her European vacation. "It was like I had some kind of terrible disease, and I couldn't figure out why. I don't know anybody with a more loving family background than I have, so I knew that didn't have anything to do with it. I was a reasonably happy person, with a good social life, so I knew it wasn't that. I didn't know what it was."

Jerilyn returned from her vacation to New York City, where she was born and raised and worked as an elementary school math teacher. She arrived determined to forget what she'd been through or at least to put it aside and move on. Almost as a strange coincidence, she returned to school at nights in pursuit of a master's degree in psychology, all the while hoping to keep her newfound fears under something resembling control.

Like most phobics, Jerilyn didn't let on what she was suffering. "I never told anybody until I was thirty," she recalls, "and because of that a lot of times it wasn't easy to explain my behavior. Every aspect of my life was affected by it. Living in New York, I knew everybody's floor in their apartment building. I would go to these extremes to avoid visiting a high floor. For some reason, the tenth floor became the cutoff point. I told myself I couldn't go to someone's apartment if they were above the tenth floor.

"I know now it was irrational," she says, "everything about it was irrational, and part of me knew it then, but you become a master of manipulation in these things. You become almost a hostage to your fears. I let it rule my life. People would invite me to dinner and I'd say, 'Hey, why don't you come over to my place instead?' Someone would have a party, and I'd cancel at the last minute. I thought about taking other jobs outside of teaching but decided against them because I knew I'd have to work in a tall office building. My world started getting smaller and smaller. In everything I did, professional and social, I had to hide behind it."

But Jerilyn slowly came out of hiding. She took a leave of absence from teaching and moved to Washington, D.C. (Jerilyn jokes that one of the reasons she moved is that the buildings in our nation's capital only go up to the twelfth floor.) The farther she got away from teaching, the more Jerilyn realized she wanted to find a new career that would make good use of the knowledge and experience gained in study for her master's degree. "As a teacher I was realizing I was only one of thousands of New York City school teachers," she explains. "It was hard to feel you were making a difference. But what I enjoyed most about teaching was the interaction. I was looking for something that would give me that interaction."

Eventually Jerilyn found herself co-leading a ten-person phobia support group, under the direction of a leading Washington-area psychiatrist. "I had no clinical experience at that time," she recalls. "I was just sort of thrust into it, acting sort of like half patient, half therapist. Basically I was just listening and talking about my own experiences, lending support, but I started to realize that I could have a profound impact on other people's lives. I thought maybe something like this would be for me."

Soon after, an article appeared in the *Washington Post*, focusing on Jerilyn and her work, spurring hundreds of inquiries about treatment groups in the area. Jerilyn then published a widely read paper in the influential *American Journal of Psychiatry*, and before she knew what hit her, she had emerged as an authority in an evolving field. "I went from someone who knew almost nothing about phobias," Jerilyn admits, "other than what I had experienced firsthand, to someone who was internationally known in less than two years." (Kind of like a guy I knew who knew nothing about weather, other than what he learned from underneath his own umbrella, and who was all of a sudden thrust in front of a television weather map.)

Jerilyn has been one of the pioneers in what has come to be known as "contextual therapy," in which the therapist seeks out a phobic situation with the patient and then helps the patient to confront that situation. "It is not our intent to teach people to ignore their fears," explains Jerilyn, "but to teach them to refocus their thinking. If we reintroduce them into the panic-causing situation, gradually and with support, we can teach them how to get control of their feelings. It's a behavioral approach, really. In my case, I learned that, despite my fears, I am not going to walk to the edge of a cliff or a building or whatever and jump off. I learned that whatever pull I was feeling, the magnet I talked about earlier, was not based on anything dangerous, and that if I just learned to live with it, I would be fine. It was frightening, but it was not dangerous. That's what we try to teach people; we teach them that their feelings, however frightening, can't hurt them."

Now, though, Jerilyn has trouble finding time to pursue the one-to-one therapy she helped to develop, with most of her work days given over to supervisory and administrative chores and to the full-time job of getting the word out, of promoting national awareness of phobia treatments through the press and through a heavy schedule of public appearances. "I miss that aspect of things, sure," she admits. "I got into this as a therapist, and there is something special about working on an individual basis, but I think I'm able to help more people by concentrating on the big picture." It is through Jerilyn's public persona as a Phobia Society of America spokesperson that we first met, as I began to appear at more and more of their luncheons and conferences. When we'd talk, I'd realize we shared an important bond, as if we'd both come through at the happy end of the same struggle.

Jerilyn is quick to offer advice to others suffering even from mild phobias. "When your phobias interfere with your life, that's when you have to go get help," she counsels. "Don't keep it to yourself. Talk to a friend, or a family member, or a clergyman. But don't stop there. Someone close to you, like a spouse or a parent, can be a good sounding board, but they can't be your therapist. You're likely to be more open and honest with someone else. Find that someone else and start talking. Find a support group in your area. We have a hopeful message at the Phobia Society: people with panic disorders and phobias need not feel alone."

It might be helpful for you to know that Jerilyn still suffers bravely through the fears that first brought her to this place in her life and career. "I still get anxious sometimes, in certain situations," she admits, "and I think I always will. But now I know how to control those anxious feelings and not run away from the situation."

Sounds good to me.

★ ★

FEAR ITSELF

★ **SHERRI JOINER**

Mt. Rainer, Maryland

Sherri Joiner is a beautiful, courageous young woman who at one difficult time in her life didn't leave her apartment for four years. I look at her phobias, at what she's been through and overcome, and my own fears seem infinitely small, almost trivial by comparison. But the most wonderful thing about Sherri, as you'll see when you meet her, is that she's been able to keep her sense of humor through it all. Despite the very real horrors she's suffered—and still suffers, to some measureable degree—Sherri Joiner can laugh at herself.

Sherri is an agoraphobic, which basically means she is afraid of leaving the house and interacting with what psychologists call "the marketplace." But actually she is afraid of a lot of things. Or, to hear her tell it, she's afraid of most things. We sat with each other at a recent Phobia Society of America function, and she told me about a magazine article she'd recently read that listed people's most common fears. "They mentioned twenty-eight different phobias," Sherri said. "You know, with the psychological names for them and everything. Well, of the twenty-eight things they mentioned, I was afraid of twenty-five of them." She paused a second or two for a quiet chuckle. "Can you imagine?" she said. "The only things I'm not afraid of are numbers and flowers, and I think it was some kind of fish."

Like most phobic people, Sherri's fears came with adulthood. As a child she says she was saddled with nothing more than the usual childhood fears—fears of what might be under the bed, of not preparing adequately for a test in school, things like that. But it was not until she was seventeen years old that Sherri experienced her first frightening panic attack, and it was unlike anything she had ever seen, heard of, or imagined.

"I was in the subway," she says of her first attack. "My heart started palpitating, I became incredibly nervous and disoriented." The memory of her first frightening experience is still fresh, the wounds not yet healed, and as Sherri tells her story I get the feeling she is living through that harrowing moment all over again. "I remember hearing people talking right next to me," she recalls, "but they looked like they were drifting away. They started fading away from me, and then their voices faded away, too. I got the shakes, and there were beads of perspiration on my forehead. I was nauseated. I remember thinking I was going to swallow my tongue. The only thing I could think to do was run, get away. I thought I was dying."

And this was only the first attack of several. Over the next two years, the panic attacks started happening in bunches—at movie theaters, in restaurants, on buses, in stores. Each time Sherri would again think she was dying, that she was having some sort of random, violent heart attack, and each time she would run from the theater or wherever she was, run as fast as she could, all the time scared and confused about what was happening to her. Between attacks, though, Sherri put aside her secret notion that she was going quietly crazy and managed to hold together the strings of an outgoing life; she even found time to get married.

But at nineteen, on a trip to the grocery store, Sherri reached the breaking point. "I started getting nervous," she recalls. "I was shaking a little, but I was still waiting my turn on line, to pay for whatever it was I was buying. I knew another attack was coming, but I thought I could get out of there and home before it got too bad. But then it came my turn to pay, and everything just exploded. It was one of the worst attacks I'd ever had. So I ran out of the store, ran all the way back home, and I didn't come back out of my apartment for four years."

Now, think about that for a minute. Four years! That's an awful long time. People go to college for four years. I try to imagine myself within the same set of walls for that long, and I don't get very far. Of course, Sherri didn't know she'd be housebound for so long at the time, only that with each day she couldn't face the fears and pressures and uncertainties of the rest of the world. Each day she retreated farther and farther into her private world, her safe world, and each passing day made it more difficult to escape. She became entrenched. "I'd still have the attacks at home," she recalled. "But at least I was someplace I was comfortable. You know, I knew where I was and everything. And after a while I knew that even though it felt like I was going to die, I wasn't going to die. I knew I would live through them."

At first, Sherri was afraid to reveal to her husband the extent of her fears. She would make up excuses each time he wanted to go out; according to her assortment of alibis, she was forever suffering from minor aches and pains and common colds. Sherri was afraid that if she let on exactly what she was feeling—the palpitating heart, the nausea, the fear of swallowing her tongue—her husband would have her committed to a mental institution. "After a while he started to catch on to what I was going through," she says now, "but only a little bit. He thought it was a mind-over-matter thing. He thought I could just tell myself to leave the house, and I'd be okay. He tried, but he didn't understand."

But the trouble was, Sherri didn't understand, either, not really. That's what happens so often in these cases, it's what happened, in a way, to me. Sherri didn't understand that what she was suffering was not a physical illness, but an emotional one. She didn't know there were others, millions of others, suffering similar attacks and fears. As her four housebound years wore on, Sherri thought she was hopelessly, desperately alone.

"Crossword puzzles, jigsaw puzzles, books, that's what kept me busy," she explains. "I would watch television, I just didn't like to see anything about people being possessed by the devil, anything like that." She laughs when she says this last part, but actually it was television that saved her life. One day, flipping the channels, she landed on a local talk show focusing on phobias. "There was a phobic person on there," she says, "talking about what I was like, what I was feeling. It was like she knew exactly what I was going through. Right then I started crying. Right then I knew I wasn't alone and that I'd be all right."

After the show, Sherri called the local station for more information. They put her in touch with Jerilyn Ross, the therapist from the Phobia Society of America you met earlier, who also appeared on the program. And after a few stops and starts, Jerilyn succeeded in helping Sherri slowly free herself from her fears.

"I don't know what would have happened if I hadn't seen Jerilyn on TV," Sherri admits softly, her voice thick with emotion, with the prospects of living still with her paralyzing fears. "I really was at the point where I had to do something. Really, I felt that if I had to spend another day confined to that apartment, going through what I was going through, I would take my life. I was fed up." Her husband was also fed up, and he moved out during the early stages of Sherri's rehabilitation. (The two have since reconciled and moved into a new apartment.) "But," Sherri insists, "you have to get fed up before you're going to get better."

And now that she is getting better, now that she's got a handle on her fears and is able to regain some sort of control over her own life, Sherri is still searching for reasons. "They still can't tell me why," she admits. "I can't help but wonder about things. I feel like I've gone through enough already, but I know that I'm not finished with it. But I do wonder, you know, 'Why me?' I mean, it happens to people who had good childhoods, people who had bad childhoods. It happens to rich people and poor people. It happens to famous people, and it happens to people nobody knows. It doesn't matter who you are or where you come from. It just happens."

That's the thing with an unrelenting phobia like Sherri's. It seems cruel and unfair and perversely random in manifesting itself. But it is people like Sherri Joiner, people able to battle their fears and fight them to a standstill (and, sometimes, to victory), who are a constant inspiration to me. If Sherri Joiner can live through and live with her fears, then so can I. And so can you.

★ ★

"My middle name is 'Avoid City.' "—
Moneta Wilkins.

BRIDGE OVER TROUBLED WATERS

★ **MONETA WILKINS**

Auburn Heights, Michigan

Bridges mean the same thing to Moneta Wilkins that they sometimes mean to me: trouble.

Add freeways and certain high buildings to the equation, and you'll get an idea of what's panicked this lovely lady during most of her adult life. Oh, yeah, sometimes escalators get to her, but only when she's going down. Up doesn't seem to bother her.

"My middle name is 'Avoid City,' " jokes Moneta. "I know all the surface routes around town, to and from work, everywhere. When I go to Canada, and I go to Canada a lot, I take the tunnel, when I go to work I take the back roads, I stay off the freeways. I can avoid everything that gives me trouble, so in a sense I've never been crippled by my fears."

But seriously, she doesn't want to live a life of avoidance, and—her middle name aside—she sought help almost immediately after her first frightening incident on the Ambassador Bridge, which runs from Detroit to Windsor, Ontario, in Canada. "I knew there was a problem right away," she recalls. "Something in me just snapped, and I knew I had to learn to deal with it. It happened a few times. I would get stuck. I couldn't go forward, I couldn't go backward, I couldn't get out of the car, and I couldn't stand to stay in the car. I'd be hysterical with fear, just screaming and crying, not able to do anything."

She discussed her problem with her gynecologist, who in turn recommended a psychiatrist, and she began therapy. "That was in the seventies," says Moneta, who is now forty-seven, "before they knew a whole lot about phobias, before they knew to desensitize patients through exposure therapy, things like that. They gave me some Valium, but I didn't think it did anything. We talked about my childhood and all that jazz."

She didn't get anywhere with this first therapist, not really, so she continued her search for proper and specific treatment for her panic disorders. She had the right idea, and she is grateful now that she knew enough as a young woman to seek help. "About the worst thing you can do with a thing like this is keep it to yourself," she says.

Every time she heard news of a new phobia clinic or a new treatment program, she would check it out. Another doctor put her on a drug called Zanax, an antianxiety drug that is commonly prescribed for phobic patients. Eventually, Moneta wound up with a group called Agoraphobics in Motion (AIM), which meets every Tuesday in a church in nearby Warren, Michigan, and things have been looking up ever since. Although AIM is peopled mostly with agoraphobics, Moneta is what you might call a "simple phobic," in that she is afraid of only one or two very specific things. "It's a wonderful group," she says, "very supportive. It helps a lot of us to know that every Tuesday, no matter what, there'll be someone there for us to talk to. Even if Christmas Eve fell on a Tuesday, there'd be someone there." Moneta says that with AIM's help she has the business with the freeways and tall buildings pretty much licked; the thing with the escalators comes and goes; and the fear of bridges, well, she says that will take some time.

"I have a support person who goes with me over the bridges once in a while," Moneta says, "but you have to do it every day, you really have to work at it if you're gonna get better, and I just can't. I'm too busy, for one thing, and also it's just too expensive. I've got to pay a toll each way, and I can't afford it. I've tried to explain to the people at the toll booths that I'm just going back and forth, trying to work out a problem, but they say that I have to pay just the same. I know that if I could get out there and work on it every day, I'd have that one licked, too." That's the way I licked my problems with bridges, as I mentioned earlier, through a consistent effort to beat this thing by building up my immune system against it. I'd go back and forth, over and back, this way and that way, several times a day, and eventually I wore my fears down to a size where I could handle them.

When Moneta has trouble on a bridge, when she's hysterical with fear and stuck in her car on an overpass somewhere, she is usually able to flag a passing car and ask someone to drive her across, even though these days something like that can be more fear-inducing than the initial fear itself. "Sure, it's a chance you take, asking perfect strangers to get into your car and help you," Moneta admits. "I could have been killed in lots of situations out there, taken advantage of in some way, but always, at the time, it seems I have no other choice. I've been lucky about that."

And she's getting better. "Once I was driving over the bridge saying to myself, 'I can't, I can't, I can't,' but I was, sure enough I was, and I still kept saying, 'I can't.' Phobics tend to be very negative about things, agoraphobics especially, about what they're not able to accomplish." Used to be Moneta knew all the trouble spots she'd pass on the way to work—there were three of them—but lately she's been able to drive right on by without any problem.

She's accomplished quite a lot, Moneta, despite her fears. She works as a certified pharmacy technician, and she sings with a group called the Don Large Singers. (Don Large, for those too young to remember, used to feature young singers on a CBS radio show called "Make Way for Youth," during the forties, fifties, and sixties.) Moneta, who sang with Don Large while she was growing up, tours the state with other alums from the program, performing in churches and schools and community theaters, passing over many a bridge along the way.

"Sometimes I'm able to go a few days without any anxious feelings," Moneta says. "I have my setbacks, I think we all have our setbacks, but I'm almost there. It is possible to recover from things like this, lots of people have. You just sometimes need other people to lean on, you need other people for support. Exposure is the most important therapy, and of course you have to believe in yourself. Lots of times I go out there and try to drive across a bridge, you know, and I'll think I'm gonna be brave, and then I'll chicken out. But you can't chicken out, not if you want to beat this thing. You have to believe in yourself."

I believe she's right.

I'VE met hundreds of people around the country with their own set of fears, big and small, and each and every one of us at one point thought that what we were suffering was as bad as it gets, that nobody could possibly be worse off than we were. Now, I'm nothing but an armchair psychologist, but it seems to me we all have a tendency to attach a self-importance to our own problems. This is not a good thing, phobicly speaking. Phobics need to know they're not alone, that there are others like them, before they can begin to accept treatment. It was that way with me, and it was that way with the three women you met in this chapter. File this thought away, for you or for a friend; you never know when it might come in handy.

That's me as the first-ever Ronald McDonald.

9 Clowning Around

I WAS destined to be a clown from the time I was born. I don't mean a circus clown or anything like that, but I've always been something of a cut-up, a character. I'm the kind of guy who loves to make people laugh, and over the years I've just sort of walked through life with a lampshade over my head. (Or a rug, if you insist.)

Even as a kid, I fit the part. I can remember the first play I ever appeared in; I was in grammar school, maybe I was five or six years old, and we put on *Billy Goat's Gruff*. I didn't play the old billy goat, or the prince; I played the troll, and the troll was the clown. You might say that was the beginning of the end for me. I played the light roles all through high school, the comic relief, and I've carried something of that with me throughout my career.

My first efforts in radio were always funny, or at least I thought they were funny. I always tried to put some kind of zinger into everything I've done, a twist, something that would take people back a little bit because it was different. That's one of the things that made the chemistry on "The Joy Boys" work so well for so long. Eddie Walker and I refused to do things the easy way, the way things were done on other shows. We were always after the bigger laugh, the bigger surprise.

"The Joy Boys" led directly to one of the big breaks in my career, and I was more surprised than anybody when it happened. The folks at the NBC television station in Washington —WRC-TV—had signed on a national kiddie show, and they tapped me to star in the thing. That's how I got to be Bozo the Clown. (You'll hear a bit more about Bozo and his creator, Larry Harmon, when I get tired of talking about myself.) At last, an honest-to-goodness clown! There was a bunch of us Bozos around the country, and we'd do the shows locally and run the same cartoons. We all learned the routine out at Larry Harmon's studios in Los Angeles, and I remember the big thrill for me was being out there on the set next to "Gunsmoke" and seeing people like James Arness walking around in their civvies. I still get a kick out of things like that.

Anyway, when I came back to Washington, I added a few twists of my own to the Bozo character. I would squeak the kids' noses, that was my trademark. I had this horn that I'd hooked onto a safety pin attached to my undershirt beneath the clown suit; I'd ask a kid his name, and then I'd give his nose a little tweak with one hand and hit my horn at the same time with the other. They loved it!

I did the show for several years, and it opened more than a few doors for me. Actually, I like to think Bozo opened some doors for a lot of people. During the early 1960s, the Soviets banned all Western journalists from Moscow for one reason or another. Everybody in network news was kind of frantic over the news embargo, when out of the blue we got a call at

My interpretation of Bozo.

NBC from the secretary of the Russian embassy. We had no idea what was up, we hoped it had something to do with a lifting of the ban, but what he wanted was tickets to the Bozo show for his kids! Now, Bozo can't take full credit, but soon after that the Russians allowed newsmen back into Moscow. I like to think that old clown had more than a little to do with closing that sad chapter in our history.

Eventually I started doing personal appearances as Bozo all over our viewing area. I even went to the White House to do my thing at a birthday party for little Caroline Kennedy. (Oh, were my feelings hurt when she didn't ask me to do a repeat performance at her wedding!) The appearances were a blast. They got me out of the studios on a regular basis, and I really got a kick out of playing to a crowd.

Once I appeared in Frederick, Maryland, at the Frederick County Fairgrounds, and I was there in my Bozo suit and Bozo Mobile. The Bozo Mobile was this jeep we had rigged as an open surrey, and usually I'd drive to personal appearances in the thing. I guess it must have been good promotion for the station to have me driving around town dressed in costume like that, in such a conspicuous vehicle.

Well, wouldn't you know it, I ran out of gas. First time it's ever happened to me, and there I am in a jeep, dressed for all the world like a clown. How's that for comic relief? So I step out onto the highway and try to flag down some help, and all these cars are going by, and no one's stopping. Station wagons filled with little kids are passing, and the kids are waving at me through the windows, and still no one's stopping. Nobody picked me up. Must be they thought it was some sort of promotion or gimmick, or maybe they just thought I was a lunatic. Who knows?

I was stranded there for going on an hour—it even started to rain—when a kind old man pulled over in his 1948 Chevy coupe to give me a lift. You should have seen this car—no upholstery on the seats inside, just springs. But I'm grateful for the lift, and I get in and I'm shivering and I'm all over the guy with thanks, but he doesn't say a thing to me. There I am, dressed as a clown, with my fiery orange hair and all, and he doesn't bat an eye. Not a word or a second look. About four miles up the road there's an Esso station, and we pull up so I can get out and get some gas, and I turn to the old man one more time to thank him again for the ride, and finally he turns to me and says, "That's all right, Mr. Bozo. Before I had my car I used to hitchhike and nobody picked me up, either."

I may not have gotten a lot of mileage out of that Bozo Mobile, but I sure get a lot of mileage out of that story.

I did a lot of personal appearances as Bozo—at shopping malls, local fairs, that sort of thing. After a while a local McDonald's restaurant asked me to appear at an opening, and before too long my Bozo was a regular fixture at area franchises. When WRC dropped Bozo—I was killed by declining ratings, if you must know—McDonald's didn't much like the idea of having to drop a successful promotion. They were hooked on clowns—they thought it was a terrific way to reach kids, and by golly it was—but I couldn't appear as Bozo once WRC canceled the show.

And so—you guessed it—Ronald McDonald was born, and

he's a direct descendent of Bozo the Clown. Actually, he came very close to being christened Donald McDonald, but Ronald sounded just a touch more natural, so we went with that. I created him for a company called GG Distributors, which owned about seventy-five McDonald's restaurants in the capital area. They kept me pretty busy, and they paid me pretty darn well for my time—$20,000 a year, which was a lot of loose change in those days. At one point, Oscar Goldstein, one of the G's in GG Distributors, took me aside to offer what I should have seen as a sweet deal. "Willard," he said to me, "McDonald's stock is gonna go public, and it's gonna be a dynamite stock." He wanted to pay my fee in stock instead of in cash.

Well, I'd seen hamburger joints come and go, and I figured two all-beef patties in the hand were worth a few in the bush. I passed on his offer. Instead I took my money one year and invested it in a company called Underwater Storage, which stored government records in these strange-looking plastic bubble bins sunk off the coast of Bermuda. Of course, with my luck, the company went belly up. (I never did find out what happened to all those government records.) If I'd listened to my friend Goldy, I'd be telling a much different story, one with a happier ending, as far as I'm concerned. I figured it out one day, and if I'd taken my fee from Goldy in stock for the four years we worked together, my McDonald's holdings would be worth something like seven million dollars. Seven million dollars! Nice work if you can get it, or if you're smart enough to take it.

Of course, my career in funny costumes doesn't begin or end with Ronald or Bozo. Give me an outfit, any outfit, and if it fits, I'll wear it. Down in Washington, they used to say, "Willard will do anything." And they were right. You wouldn't believe some of the crazy promotional stunts they had me do, but I always figured, What the heck, if somebody think's it'll help the station, or the show, or my career, then I'm willing to give it a go.

I carried that attitude with me to the "Today" show. One time I did the weather dressed as Carmen Miranda, and I'm still living it up trying to live that one down. Nearly every day I hear from people around the country who fondly re-

One of my greatest hits, as Carmen Miranda on August 22, 1983.

member that broadcast. I'm known for that more than any single thing I've done on the air. It was absolutely, totally outlandish, and the thing that was so funny about it was it caught people off guard. It ran the gamut from the ridiculous to the sublime, and then it turned around and ran back again. Almost every major paper in the country ran my picture the next morning; my scrapbooks are bulging with shots of me in a headpiece made of plastic fruit! I love to pull stunts like that, to put some kind of zip into what I do. Like dressing up as Boy Willard, or sparring with a kangaroo, or going in for a swim on a beach remote. It keeps things interesting.

Of course, sometimes circumstances force me to mug it up a bit for the cameras. I'll do anything in a pinch, to get out of a jam, especially if I can have some fun with it. Like the time I left my hair in New York, when I was flying to Los Angeles to appear on "The Joan Rivers Show." Now, if you know me, you know that sometimes I wear designer hair, and sometimes I don't; I kinda like to have it on, though, when I make

"Boy Willard."

a major national appearance. On a personal appearance, one to one, I'll go topless, but on national television I like to have my security blanket snugly in place.

What happened in this instance was I was rerouted to Pittsburgh (the joke there is that the rerouting of airline traffic is that city's biggest source of tourism), and there was no way I could retrieve my hair and make it out to Los Angeles in time for the show. So I called my office and had them arrange for a Prince Charming costume, complete with a festive hat, to be waiting in my dressing room at Fox Broadcasting. I figured the least I could do was ham it up a little bit; after all, the Fox Broadcasting Company didn't want some overweight bald man on their show, they wanted a clown. I gave 'em a clown. (I also gave Joan a thrill when I doffed my hat to reveal a heart I had drawn on my shiny bald head. That was good for a few laughs.)

Look, I've met a few clowns in my day. Mostly they've tended to wear funny suits (these guys at NBC wear this gray pin-striped job that's just a riot), and they do their act under the big tops of the Capitol Building or the White House. And yes, once in a while, I just want to gag on some of their gags. I know, I know, it's a cheap line, but anything for a laugh, I always say, and so say the first-class characters you'll meet here.

★ ★

"When I go off to the big circus in the sky, I'll be smiling inside." —*Larry "Bozo" Harmon.*

MY OLD PAL BOZO

★ **LARRY HARMON**

Los Angeles, California

More than anyone else you'll meet in this book, Larry Harmon changed my life. For those few of you who don't know Larry's story, he is the brains and heart and funny bone behind Bozo the Clown. That's right, Larry Harmon is your old pal Bozo, and his gift of love and laughter is something I will cherish for the rest of my life.

Not many people know this, but Bozo is approaching his fiftieth birthday. Larry created the character back in 1940, as a high school student in Cleveland, Ohio, to complement his dance club act in clubs and dance halls and community fairs in the Ohio area. "I'd always been an entertainer," Larry recalls, "and I was looking to come up with a character, some creation, that would perpetuate myself, something that would outlive me. I wanted to come up with something that would last."

One of the things that always impressed me about Larry and his success is that he went about the creation of Bozo systematically—he went to the library and researched some of the classic entertainment characters throughout history. He knew what he wanted and approached it from a thinking man's perspective. "What I found was that the clown, or what we now think of as the clown, has been around since the beginning," Larry says. "You know, there'd always been a court jester, some character given to warmth and laughter. I came out of those books and decided my character should be a clown."

Larry's clown—named Bozo for the way it sounds, and, he says, because "Bozo is Bozo in any language, English, French, Japanese, anything"—became a big hit around Cleveland, and when Larry was summoned to serve in World War II, he packed along his clown outfit and strutted his stuff wherever and whenever the opportunity arose. It was during the war that Larry met and impressed the likes of Eddie Cantor and Al Jolson, who later coaxed him out to the West Coast at the war's end. Larry enrolled at USC, where he was a drum major in the school marching band and studied to become a doctor, but his Bozo antics were distracting him from his books. Apart from his clowning and his studies, he took bit roles in many films of the late 1940s (he worked with stars like Clark Gable and Spencer Tracy) and continued with his music.

In the middle 1950s, he talked his way onto KTLA-TV with an afternoon kiddie show, and the rest, as they say, is history. The show was an instant hit in the Los Angeles area, and Larry sought to take advantage of his success and syndicate the program nationwide. The trouble was, in those days there were no such things as satellite or taped feeds, so the only way to make the show available on a national basis was to "franchise" it—that is, to set up local, stand-alone Bozo shows operating with local talent in each market. "I remember the first station I sold on the franchising concept was

WPIX-TV in New York," Larry says, "and the general manager there couldn't understand that I wouldn't be doing the show. I gave him my pitch, did the Bozo routine, and he said, 'Okay, you're hired,' and I said, 'No, you don't understand. I don't want to do the show.' And he said, 'Well, if you don't want to do the show, then why are you wasting my time?' It took a while, but I finally convinced him I could train one of his announcers to do the show as well as I could. That was the beginning."

Larry went through the same routine at WRC-TV in Washington, where I was working as a staff announcer. After Los Angeles and New York, we were one of the first stations he approached. Larry sold the station managers on the concept and tapped me to carry on his young tradition to capital-area kiddies. He told my boss he could transform me into a Bozo as original as the original, sort of like Professor Henry Higgins molding Eliza Doolittle into his fair lady—my fair Bozo. He's quite a salesman, my friend Larry, because my boss bought the idea and agreed that Larry could turn me into more of a clown than I already was. All you had to do was look at Larry and you knew he'd deliver on his promise. All you had to do was look at me and you knew, well, at least he'd have something to work with. I remember flying out to Los Angeles three days after I was married (come to think of it, Mary's friends were all telling her she had married a clown), and Larry met me at the airport in a big red Cadillac with leopardskin upholstery and spent the next week or so training me on some of the finer points of what he likes to call "Bozology."

By the time we were through I could Bozo with the best of them, even Larry. I had the walk, the talk, the look, and the feel of the character down pat. I've often thought it would be a lot of fun to line up all of the Bozos—at one point, Larry had original shows running in 183 television markets—to see if viewers could spot the Bozo from their hometown area. I know Larry would get a kick out of something like that. (Incidentally, Bozo is still running in twelve markets, most notably on superstation WGN in Chicago, making it the longest-running television show in history; the original Chicago Bozo, a nice man named Bob Bell, recently retired after twenty-three years in the role.)

Larry has turned on his success with Bozo to become one of Hollywood's most successful producers (he's now looking to syndicate some two hundred old Bozo shows to a late night audience under the title "Bedtime for Bozo") and one of the most sought-after speakers on the lecture circuit. In and out of his Bozo garb, he is known and loved all over the world. He tells this wonderful story about the time he was honored nearly twenty years ago at a university in Thailand and answered one question about his religious beliefs with his characteristic good cheer. "I answered that my church is laughter," Larry recalls, "and that got a nice response, but what I remember most is a well-dressed young man from India who stood up and said, you know, in a rich Indian accent, 'This church of laughter you speak about, how can we join?' "

Many of you might recall Larry's famous bid, as Bozo, for the presidency in 1984. Yes, that presidency. I remember his appearance on the "Today" show during his campaign, and I was ready to laugh along at what I thought was a pretty good practical joke. (After all, it is funny, the sight of a man in a clown outfit running for the highest office in the land; it also says a lot about the men and women who seek the position without benefit of a costume.) But then Larry turned up in the NBC studios, and I think we were all terrifically impressed with his message.

"My platform was peace, love, understanding, and laughter," Larry says now. "How do you fight that one?" His true mission, though, was to get out the vote, and when the results were in, it appears he succeeded in his effort. "I had heard a statistic, something like one-half of the people in this country don't vote," Larry explains. "Fifty percent! In a democracy! That's embarrassing. I thought a good way to bring attention to the election, to get people to vote, was to run for the office myself." According to Larry's tally, nearly two million people took the time and trouble to vote for Larry/Bozo as a write-in candidate, an astonishing figure when you stop to think that Larry campaigned in his Bozo costume throughout, and that he only announced his candidacy in March of that election year. I didn't bother to check his figures, because if you ask me, he came up a winner.

Larry agrees: "As far as I'm concerned, I won that election," he says. "I booked the ballroom in the Washington Press Club, because I wanted to do it up right, but the members of the press didn't know what to make of my candidacy. They didn't know if it was a joke or what to make of the whole thing. But as I went on, I heard from a lot of people, from the networks, from the major newspapers, a lot of people, and they all told me I would have been a fine president. All these politicians talk baloney, and they think it's food for thought, and my message made a lot of sense to a lot of people. Two million people is a lot of people. That's probably more votes than Abraham Lincoln got."

Larry takes a special pride in the fact that he's left his mark on this earth. "I'm in the dictionary," he says. "Go ahead, look it up. 'Bozo' is in the dictionary. I've become part of the language." Sure enough, he has, or at least his character has, but to hear Larry talk you'd think he's bucking for a few more entries in *Webster's*—he describes his emotions with words like "Bozaic" or "Boziphorous," and for some reason I know exactly what he's talking about.

But on a serious note, Larry Harmon has truly made a ding-dong-dandy difference in all of our lives. "When I go off to the big circus in the sky, I'll be smiling inside," he says, sincere as could be. "I'll know that I've left these size eighty-three, triple-A footprints behind me and that somehow, somewhere, somebody called Bozo will be walking around in my shoes saying, 'J-u-u-u-u-u-u-st keep on laughing!' "

I'm proud to have filled Larry Harmon's size eighty-three shoes, and I know there are some 250 Bozos like me who share that pride. Because of Larry, all of us—those who've worn his costume and those who've smiled along with the men who have—have learned to j-u-u-u-u-u-st keep on laughing.

Thank you Larry Harmon, our old pal Bozo.

★ ★

*Tammy and Tommy Parish poking
fun at one of my favorite institutions.*

THESE KIDS RAN OFF WITH THE CIRCUS (AND THEY'RE NEVER COMING BACK!)

★ TOMMY & TAMMY PARISH

Neodesha, Kansas

Hung on the wall of their cramped living quarters aboard the Ringling Bros. and Barnum & Bailey Circus train, husband and wife clowns Tommy and Tammy Parish proudly display the "Clown's Prayer," a credo that is also worn proudly in their hearts:

As I stumble through this life,
Help me to create more laughter than tears,
Dispense more happiness than gloom,
Spread more cheer than despair.

More than eight years after running away with the circus, the couple's prayers are still answered every day with a broad, exaggerated smile. "It's a responsibility, when you put on that makeup," says Tammy. "It's a license to have fun and do anything you want, but there is also a responsibility to a long tradition, to what people expect from you. I think both of us take that responsibility very seriously."

They do, although when you see them perform you'll be having too much fun to notice. I first met this dynamic duo several years ago at the Ringling Bros. Clown College in Sarasota, Florida, the country's only full-fledged training ground for would-be clowns. If memory serves, a bunch of us were stuffing our clown selves into a tiny clown car—a timeless circus gag that never fails to get a laugh—and I was probably taking up more than my share of space.

A visit to the clown college is a special thrill for an old clown like me. It's a magical place, but the most impressive thing about it is the spirit of love and laughter that permeates the grounds. It sounds corny, but it's a spirit you can taste and feel all around you when you're there. The stuff is painted on in thick, double coats on the college walls, and if you stick around long enough, you'll be jolly with the fumes. The most impressive thing about Tommy and Tammy is their shared passion for circus and clowning tradition, for making people laugh, and for each other. I get a big kick in the pants just watching them work together.

Technically speaking, Tommy and Tammy were not high school sweethearts, even though the kind folks in the Ringling Bros. promotion department like to bill them as such. It is nice, though, to think that they were, which is probably why the circus got carried away with the idea. Well, okay, maybe they were each somebody's sweetheart in high school, but it seems they weren't each other's. "We've known each other since we were so big," Tommy says, his open palm facing down at about waist level. "We'd go on double dates together in high school, but one of us was in the front seat, and the other was in the back."

"He means we were each with other dates," Tammy explains. "We were junior college sweethearts, really."

Growing up in the small town of Neodesha, Kansas, the two would find themselves traveling to nearby Wichita, Tulsa, and Kansas City every time the circus came to town. "I'd never miss a circus when I was a kid," Tommy admits, "and the part of the circus I loved most was the clowns. That's what I wanted to be. That was always my dream." They were circus junkies. The two developed their shared interests in local clown clubs, performing at birthday parties and hospitals in their hometown area. They learned to ride unicycles together. (Now there's a great way to get to know your mate!) Neither had any idea they'd be able to turn their love of clowning into a profession, until Tommy, then a student at Independence Community College ("regular people college," he calls it), saw an article on the clown college in a Ringling Bros. circus program. He decided to apply.

Tommy, now twenty-eight, was relentlessly creative in his pursuit of admission into clown college, where some three to five thousand applicants vie for some sixty spots. "He wrote to them pretty much every day for a whole year," recalls Tammy, "on things like shopping bags and toilet paper, anything to get their attention." One of Tommy's most compelling pleas for entry came in the form of a life-size poster of a clown, except when you looked at it closely you saw the lines on the drawing were made up of one long, neatly lettered sentence explaining why he'd make a boffo clown. "I wore them down," Tommy says of his campaign. "They had to let me in."

"It was a lot more work than I thought it would be," Tommy admits. "I thought there'd be these big encyclopedias of gags, and you'd just take one down and look up a gag or a prop and take it from there. I thought the props would all be made for you, the gags all written, and you'd just study hard and learn what they had to teach you. But that's not the way it is at all, and it turns out writing your own gags and creating your own props are some of the best parts of this whole business."

Tammy, twenty-seven, followed close on Tommy's clown heels, enrolling in the next year's clown college class. When she graduated from the extensive ten-week program, with elaborate training in the arts of juggling, stilt walking, prop making, and costuming, she joined her husband on Ringling Bros.' Clown Alley, and the two have made the circus their life and life-style ever since. In one of their very first gags as a husband-and-wife team, they cast themselves as a newlywed clown couple in a routine that won the laugh track of traditionally married adults in every city they played.

"People always ask us how we're able to start a marriage on the road like this," Tammy says, "how we're able to keep it up, you know, live a normal life and everything. But to us this is normal. We don't know any other way of being together, any other way of life. The circus is like a miniworld, and we live a very normal life within that world."

"I think we both thrive on it," Tommy admits, "on moving into a different city all the time, being on the road. We plan to do this all of our lives. Our home is the circus, and when we're on the road, which is pretty much all of the time, it's not important where we're playing. It's good to know where you're going, but we never know where we've been, that's one of the lines we use around here. Usually we know where we're at. They give us these route cards that tell us what cities we'll be in, but what's important is that we're with the circus. It doesn't matter where we are beyond that."

The Parishes live in a cozy state car aboard the circus train, equipped with all the comforts of your basic studio apartment. It's a tight fit, but they say they manage things just fine, that there's more than enough room for the two of them and their two dogs. (The pooches appeared with them in one very funny, very clever gag from a recent tour.) Tommy and Tammy take their meals on the circus train's "pie car" or from the lunch truck that turns up in each city, although they frequently steal away in their new van for a quiet meal in a nice restaurant. "We bought the van to give us some more time to ourselves," Tammy says, "and now we drive ourselves from stop to stop. We'll always live on the train, but you see more of the country when you drive at your own pace. Plus it gives us time away from everyone else."

Tommy says that an open door in their circus train quarters means a steady stream of visitors, other clowns mostly. "It's nice," he admits, "and it's part of what makes the place special, but we could use more time alone."

But the times with their circus colleagues have often proved the most memorable on the tour. Like the time a runaway baby elephant chased a show girl backstage, through a cement wall or two and into the shower. ("The only thing that stopped him," Tammy says, "was a wall of mirrors. Suddenly this frightened baby elephant was looking right at another frightened baby elephant, and the poor thing was mesmerized.") Or the time the unit was snowed in for three shows in Norfolk, Virginia. With the same audience. ("There was a snow emergency or something," Tommy recalls, "and they weren't letting people leave. We stayed there the whole time, something like ten hours. I think everyone there had a special time, being shut in like that with the circus. There was even a baby born in the building that day.") And of course the time the rubber-faced master Red Skelton stopped in during a Kansas City appearance and took the entire clown unit out to dinner after the show. (Tammy: "He took us to his favorite barbecue joint in Kansas City, a great place, and it was just three hours of gags, one after another. It was an incredible night.")

The circus, particularly The Greatest Show on Earth put on by Ringling Bros. and Barnum & Bailey Circus, has given Tommy and Tammy Parish a lot of memories. And it's taken good care of them. They're two of the more popular and memorable clowns on the circus tour, and Tommy was recently made boss clown of the twenty-five clowns on the tour with him. As boss clown, Tommy sees to it that all the clown gags and routines are brought off as planned and on schedule, that every clown is carrying his weight. Whenever time allows, he and Tammy put their rubber noses to the grindstone to come up with new material; sometimes it takes longer than a year to plan and stage a simple three-minute routine, allowing for time to make new costumes and build new props.

"We borrow ideas wherever we can," Tommy says. "We're always working on something new. I'm always watching old movies of people like Chaplin, Buster Keaton, Harold Lloyd, people like that, trying to come up with a new twist to an old routine. I even borrowed my hair from Alfalfa," he says, referring to the old *Our Gang* character. (Tommy's bright orange wig sprouts an inventive flower of stand-up hair; he even cuts holes in his hats so the thing has a chance to poke its way through.)

"I remember as a kid I would pick out one or two clowns

and follow them throughout the circus," Tammy says. "I think a lot of people do that, and that means you always have to be completely within character because someone, somewhere, is watching your every move. It's a special kick when someone picks you out, and I've been lucky to have lots of little kids decide I'd be the one they'd follow throughout the show. Sometimes they write to you, and when they do, you know, it just gets to you. There's nothing like a little scrawled letter from a kid you've touched. How can you not answer a letter like that? I've been corresponding with some kids for years now; some are getting ready to graduate high school."

That's what they're here for, Tommy and Tammy Parish. They're here to reach down into their hearts and pass along a piece of magic to perfect strangers. "You go out there, and all you see is this sea of faces," Tommy says, "so many faces. Sometimes it can be overwhelming. So what you have to do is pick out one special face, and play to that. You have to make it more personal."

"Sometimes you even find a little kid who's so precious you end up playing to him all night," Tammy kicks in. "You know, every time you pass by his seat, you send some special magic in his direction. And the nice thing is, everybody in that area responds the same way. They all think you're playing to them, which is the best part."

I think I know exactly what she means.

★ ★

PUT ON A HAPPY FACE

★ **DON BASHAM**
Louisville, Kentucky

Most of the clowns I've worked with—you know, Bryant and Jane and the rest—have been of the professional variety. Chances are most of the clowns you've seen have been performing on television or under one big top or another. But there is a dedicated group of community clowns around this

Don "Buttons" Basham.

country, plain folk like you and me who visit schools and children's hospitals and retirement homes, doling out smiles to the people who need them most.

Don Basham is just such a clown, has been for about a dozen years. Don is a Shriner, specifically a member of Louisville's Kosair Shrine, a fraternal organization of roughly five thousand members given to the pursuit of good deeds and good times. (Shriners, you'll note, are the folks who attend meetings and functions with the black-tasseled red fezzes, a tradition for which some members receive a good share of grief.) The Kosair Shrine is the only shrine in the country that supports its own independent hospital—the Kosair Children's Hospital, with a record of some $16 million in endowments—but it is one of several with a thriving and lively clown unit. The Kosair Funsters, which Don has headed for the past two years, boasts twenty active members, each of whom makes a personal clowning appearance about once a week. As a unit, the Funsters often perform at parades and other large events; I've seen them go about their collective funny business at Louisville's annual Pegasus Festival and Parade, which kicks off each year's Kentucky Derby celebration, and—believe me—these Funsters know how to have a good time. But more than that, and I speak from first-hand experience here, Don and his friends do important

167

work, they bring some sunshine into lives temporarily darkened by shadow. Let me tell you, I've visited my share of hospitals and children's homes and retirement homes, and it's the most exciting and rewarding way for a performer to reach out and touch another human being. We need more one-to-one entertainers like Don Basham in my neighborhood.

"When I got started, I knew nothing at all about clowning," Don admits in a voice with just enough of a Kentucky twang to it to let you know where he's coming from. "I'd never even used makeup before. Some of the older fellows had to teach me how to put it on, how to act, how to create a costume. I had to learn the whole thing from scratch."

But the distance from scratch to where he is now is not as far as Don Basham first thought. "It comes natural once you get going," he says. "It comes easy, almost. I mean, the hard part is getting ready. It can take me an hour and a half to put my makeup and costume on, sometimes longer. But once you're all made up and dressed, it's almost like everything else disappears. I live my work, day and night, but when I put on that clown outfit I can be anything, do anything. I'm a clown, and nothing else matters when you're dressed up like that. I can forget whatever's bothering me and vent all my frustrations and hostilities in a very positive way."

Don manages an office for the United States Army Corps of Engineers, pretty serious doings for a man who spends his free time in baggy clothes and white face. "The people who work for me can say they work for a clown without fear," Don jokes. In his office, over his desk, Don keeps a portrait of himself in clown garb, so the engineers on his staff always know what sort of person they're dealing with. "Things can get pretty hectic and crazy at work, and it helps if we all remember we've got other things going on outside the office," he says. "It helps us put things in perspective."

The twenty members of the Kosair Funsters range from young adult to retirement age; at forty, Don falls somewhere in the middle. Among them you'll find lawyers and doctors and accountants and local businessmen. The Funsters operate under an annual budget of $4,000, but members pay for their own appearance-related expenses and for their own costumes. (A good pair of clown shoes costs between $150 and $170.) "I'm always looking for new costumes," says Don, who uses a feather duster as a trademark prop and who goes by the clown name of "Buttons." "I think we all look at some of the Ringling Bros. clowns when they come into town, and we just drool over their costumes. Everything is new and tailored and perfect, and here we are just putting together what we can."

But just as clothes don't make the man, they don't necessarily make the clown. "Makeup is the most important thing," insists Don. "Your appearance, the way you look, is really gonna make or break you as a clown. You don't want your makeup to look grainy or runny, you don't want to look cheap and shoddy or thrown together, unless of course you're a tramp clown. But there's something very sad about a clown whose makeup is poorly applied or whose wig doesn't sit right on his head. Really, I don't think your antics or shenanigans or whatever are nearly as important as the way you look."

The way he looks can sometimes turn a few heads, especially when he's driving to a personal appearance. "I get dressed at home," Don says, "we all do, and sometimes we'll get some funny looks at a red light or something like that. Sometimes some kids will catch your eye, and they'll do a double take and start beating on the car windows, and then they'll get their parents to turn around, and before you know it everybody is beating on the windows." Kind of reminds me of the story I told earlier, about the time I was stranded in Bozo garb coming home from a personal appearance in my Bozo Mobile.

Well, the double takes sometimes become triple and quadruple jobs when the Funsters pack up their yucks and guffaws for the annual Southwestern Shrine Clown Convention. "You can imagine the looks we get at the hotel when someone steps into an elevator full of clowns," Don says. One time, when the convention was held at the Peabody Hotel in Memphis, Tennessee, a resort famous for its ducks and fountain in the main hotel lobby, Don says he and his funny-faced colleagues shared the elevators with a gaggle of waddling webbed-foots. What I would have given for a glimpse of the wide-eyed hotel guests who stepped into one of those elevators!

Yet for all of the second looks he inspires, Don "Buttons" Basham wouldn't have things any other way. "I think I look at my children differently now that I'm clowning," admits Don, whose wife and two little girls sometimes assist on his clowning missions. "When I visit these kids at the hospitals and you see them in all kinds of conditions, newborn babies with birth defects or victims of child abuse or accidents or whatever, I'm just very thankful that my two kids are healthy and safe at home.

"You know, I walk into some of these hospital rooms, and I see these little kids with all these wires hooked up to them, you know, the intravenous and everything, and it just breaks my heart. And then there's that second or two when maybe I can get them to smile, or to laugh, or to forget what they're going through. That's it for me."

I'VE learned a lot during my many years in clowning, whether as Bozo or Ronald or Carmen. I did most of my work as a clown during a very turbulent time in our nation's history—the 1960s. Everywhere I went I was so impressed with what you're able to accomplish behind a clown's heavy makeup, particularly during that period of strong racial tension and violent reaction to our involvement in the Vietnam War.

When you put on a clown suit, or any costume for that matter, you put on a mask. You have no identity. You're not a Jew, you're not a Protestant, you're not a Catholic. You're not a Communist or a capitalist, a Republican or Democrat, left or right, right or wrong. You're a clown, and it's as simple as that. You're neutral, and you stand for fun and love and warmth and all sorts of good things. You're in a make-believe world, and it's a special place to be because there's a certain magic in it.

And part of that magic is that you can strip yourself of labels, all labels, and when labels disappear you strip away at prejudice. You can really communicate with people on a beautiful level when you don't give them a chance to form any preconceived notions about who you are or what you stand for. It's a lesson I've always been grateful for, and I try to put it to work for me at every chance, even now that I've stepped out of my traditional clown costumes for good (or so it appears).

Clowning's been good to me, in all its many forms, let me tell you. It's like that song "Make 'Em Laugh," which Donald O'Connor sang in *Singin' in the Rain:* be the silly ass and you'll always travel first class. Well, this silly ass is plum proud to stand as living proof of truth in advertising.

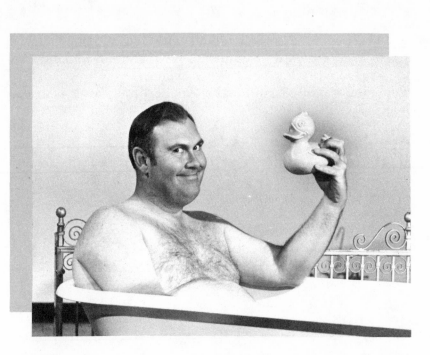

I love a good cause. Won't you join me in helping to save the rubber duck from extinction!

10 Helping Hands Across America

CHARITY begins at home, and you'll find the very best of the do-unto-others bunch in my American neighborhood.

Because of who I am and what I do, I am often asked to preside over some charitable event or another—to emcee a community awards program, host a fund-raising dinner, or chair an advisory board—and, when asked, I am more often than not thrilled to make room on my calendar. Sometimes I get paid for my helping hand and sometimes I don't, but for the most part I do what I can because I was brought up to believe that when you've got it good you've got to spread some of it around. I'm the first in line to give something back to the people who've helped put me where I am today. Besides, I'm an easy mark for a good cause, and this country is full of 'em.

One of the causes I get behind in a big way—if you'll indulge me here for just a moment—is the plight of the American Indian, because I think the generic paleface has given him a raw deal over the past few centuries and because I firmly believe that it is through the Native American Indian that we can best understand the land underneath our feet and all who've trod here before us. We've almost lost the American Indian and his way of life, and I and a lot of people are doing our darnedest to preserve and restore what's left. So much for my one plug for one of the many groups in need of our collective attention; let's get on with the business at hand.

It's still true that if you want something done right, you've got to do it yourself. I know when I believe in something I've got to give it my all; I switch into turbo and go full speed ahead. I think we're all that way, to a certain extent. You've got to get fed up or steamed enough to make a difference, or you've got to care so deeply about a thing that you do whatever it takes to see it through. I'm not talking here about giving money, although there are wonderful things to be said about charitable donations. (I, for one, can itemize my way through these new tax laws with the best of them.) No, the real difference comes from the folks who give their time and their heart.

Every once in a blue moon I'll run across a rare and special individual who's given his or her life to making things better for others. It's usually the case that what they're working for (or against, as the case may be) is something that's struck close to home, something that's made such an impact on a personal level that they get involved in the biggest of ways. It's a thing to see, believe me, and I want to share a piece of that with you here.

The buck really stops with the four good people you'll meet in this chapter, each one of them a precious national resource who's put in long, hard hours filling a desperate need, each one of them getting involved at the hands-on

173

level. They saw a way to make a difference, they gave it their best, and their efforts are just plum overflowing with good-will and good cheer. It's right neighborly of them, if I do say so myself, and the world would be a far better place if we could all follow their lead.

★ ★

Sister Mary Kathleen at Casa de los Niños.

YOU'D BE AMAZED WHAT A LITTLE LOVE CAN DO

★ **SISTER MARY KATHLEEN CLARK**

Tucson, Arizona

Somebody should make a movie about Sister Mary Kathleen Clark's life and work, with somebody wonderful like Katharine Hepburn in the title role. It could be sort of the distaff version of Spencer Tracy's *Boys Town,* except that this time around, the young charges wouldn't be juvenile delinquents, they'd be good kids who've been dealt lousy hands, the victims of child abuse and neglect. Sister Kathleen puts a roof over their heads, clothes on their backs, hot meals in their bellies, and good values in their hearts, while their parents get their lives in order. I'd be first in line for the premiere.

The best part about a story like this is that it's true. Since 1973, more than sixteen thousand Tucson-area infants and children have received shelter, food, clothing, and care at a fantastic children's crisis-care center called Casa de los Niños, which, pardon my Spanish, roughly means House of the Children. In any language, the place is a working miracle. I've seen their operation on more than one occasion, and each time I'm taken by the spirit and caring that keeps the place running, a spirit and caring you can trace right back to Sister Kathleen.

When they opened their doors, Sister Kathleen described the facility as a crisis nursery. It was the first one like it in the country, providing a temporary haven to children of troubled families. Now I'm told it's been the model for some thirty-five others, nationwide, which is an indication of Casa de los Niños' runaway success; imitation is the sincerest form of flattery.

Casa de los Niños was born in a time when drug use and abuse was even more prominent among young people than it is today, when the looser life-styles of the 1960s threatened to change the foundations on which many young families were built. It was a free-wheeling time, and many little people were brought into this world by parents who had neither the ability nor the inclination to care for them.

"We were seeing a lot of children of drug addicts," recalls Sister Kathleen, who was working at the time in an administrative capacity at nearby St. Joseph's Hospital, after a long stint as a registered nurse at another local hospital, St. Mary's. "I was shocked at some of the suffering and neglect we were seeing among babies and small children of drug users. What I wanted to know was, if we could provide a place where people could bring their children in times of crisis, would the young community respond? If such a place existed, would they use it?"

The stories Sister Kathleen tells about this time and place are both disturbing and frightening. She talks about how small children were being given glue to sniff to keep them quiet while their parents were tripping on LSD, about babies being placed to sleep in unlighted gas ovens so parents wouldn't be disturbed by their noise. "Children were being left tied to the clotheslines," Sister Kathleen says, her voice choking on the memory, "like a dog on a leash." Other children, of emotionally or maritally troubled parents, were being abused, battered, and neglected in increasing numbers. I listen to the horrors Sister Kathleen saw in those days, and my skin turns all kinds of the wrong color; it shocks me that people can treat their own children that way, and, lucky for all of us, it shocked Sister Kathleen as well. Something, she thought, just had to be done, and thankfully the Tucson community responded to her solution. Sister Kathleen was generously assisted in her ground-breaking and trailblazing efforts by a young biker couple, who canvassed the area and spread the good word about the services the Casa de los Niños shelter could provide. "I can't stress how valuable their first contacts were to the ultimate success of our dream," Sister Kathleen says. "Without them I don't think we would have been so readily accepted."

But the shelter was accepted with open arms, and today Casa de los Niños provides temporary shelter to children in crisis from birth to age eleven. It is a nonprofit, nonsectarian, nondenominational facility to prevent child abuse and neglect, and to assist and counsel mothers and other family members on the basics of good child care. "When we started out, we were just kind of baby-sitting the little toddlers for as long as the parents would let us keep them," Sister Kathleen admits, "but it's evolved over the years to something much, much more than that. Today we've got forty-five paid personnel, and we're able to care for about forty children at a time. We even started a school, for some of the children who are there for longer periods, like two or three months, with two full-time teachers."

Tender loving care like this doesn't come cheap; Casa de los Niños runs on an annual operating budget of $1.2 million, all of which is privately generated. The place has grown to include five buildings, covering nearly half a city block, and Sister Kathleen would like to see the home grow even bigger, as the need (unfortunately) demands. You can tell just by looking at the place that the good people at Casa de los Niños have taken great pains to ensure the facility has a homey, lived-in feeling. There's a grassy yard, and toys and swings, and pretty much everything a kid would need to feel at home. In the main building, there's a thick carpet, a fireplace, comfortable couches, even a parakeet in a cage. "It looks just like any other house on the block," Sister Kathleen says. "That's what we like about it."

Everyone in and around Tucson has a kind word to say about Case de los Niños, and about Sister Kathleen, indications both that the project has seeped into community consciousness. It's gotten so I can't even pass through the state of Arizona without someone pointing out the new wonders taking place in Sister Kathleen's backyard, and I feel, by extension, a part of all the excitement.

As I mentioned earlier, Casa de los Niños is entirely dependent on private donations. "You'd be surprised, but most of our support comes from the middle class and the poor," Sister Kathleen lets on. "We get a lot of donations from local churches and university fraternities, places like that." The playground equipment, for example, was paid for by a group of ex-convicts looking to give area children a better life than they had as children.

The drug problem hasn't disappeared entirely over the years (Sister Kathleen reports that the home still treats children who are born addicted to crack and coke), but it is no longer the leading cause of nonaccidental injuries in the Casa de los Niños population. Today the shelter houses physically and sexually abused children in greater numbers than ever before. "What we see today is only the tip of the iceberg," Sister Kathleen acknowledges. "There's just so much that doesn't get to us that it makes you wonder. We're able to do good work, but we're seeing only a small slice of the population in need. We could do so much more."

Most of the children passing through Casa de los Niños stay for only a few weeks, while troubled parents seek help elsewhere, although some stay longer. (Occasionally, an infant child is abandoned on the doorsteps of the home.) The facility also offers long-term support. "We encourage parents to return with their children," Sister Kathleen says, "even if they're no longer having problems."

Sister Kathleen, who is a member of the order of the Sisters of St. Joseph of Carondelet, lives on the premises at Casa de los Niños, although to her it's more than a place of residence. "It's become a way of life," she admits. Her boundless devotion to the children of her community has not gone without notice; she has been named Woman of the Year by the Tucson Advertising Club, and she has been awarded the National Jefferson Award and the Book of Golden Deeds Award. The honors and citations mean a great deal to her, Sister Kathleen says, because they are an indication of the high value and concern people place on the well-being of children.

"Some of the horrors we see, you have to think of them in a legal sense," Sister Kathleen says, "otherwise it's just devastating. You have to think of it in terms of how the law thinks of it, because to think of some of these things in human terms is just overwhelming." She pauses to catch her breath, and you get the sense that, even after all these years, what she sees every day of her life still gets to her. She continues: "But people are coming to us, voluntarily most times, they know about us, and that makes me feel like we've accomplished something. Kids seem to know it when they walk in our doors that this is the casa, this is home."

Home sweet home.

* *

THE HOUSE THAT LOVE BUILT
★ JIM MURRAY
Rosemont, Pennsylvania

Here's a guy who deserves some kind of medal for what he's done. Actually, there is already a monument to his efforts in place, but he helped to put it there, and it is this

Jim Murray with Kim Hill and yours truly at a Ronald McDonald House dedication.

living, breathing, working monument to Jim Murray's vision and dedication for which he should be honored.

Jimmy Murray's got a heart of gold. (He's also one of the nicest, most giving people I've had the sincere pleasure to meet.) More than any other individual, he is the blood, sweat, and tears behind the successful development of the more than one hundred Ronald McDonald Houses across the country (maybe I should say he's got a heart of golden arches), the safe and peaceful havens built for parents and families of terminal and seriously ill children in affiliation with adjacent hospitals. There's no other national program like it in the country, and much of the credit—try as he might to deflect it onto other worthy shoulders—has got to go to Jimmy.

Here's the story:

In the early 1970s, a brave and beautiful little girl named Kim Hill was diagnosed at the age of three with acute lymphatic leukemia. (You had a chance to visit with Kim a little bit earlier in the book.) Kim's father, Fred Hill, was working as a wide receiver for the Philadelphia Eagles football team, and some of his teammates and New Jersey neighbors decided to put their heads together to help raise some much needed money. Jimmy entered the picture as the Eagles' assistant public relations director, and under him the team launched it's first heartfelt community effort in a campaign christened "Eagles Fly for Leukemia."

179

"Out of that mustard seed came a whole team effort," Jimmy recalls. "We'd never seen the whole team, the whole community, rally around a cause like that. Little Kimmie Hill was the inspiration, and there were other children who inspired us as we went along. But as we got deeper into it, we saw that so much money was needed in so many different areas. We dedicated ourselves to something that turned out much bigger than we thought it would."

Jimmy started asking around town to determine where the group's energies would be best directed, and he heard about something called a "life island," or an isolation room being built on the cancer ward of a local hospital. The rooms provided a sterile atmosphere in which parents could be with their children on the ward and came with a price tag of $50,000. "I went back to Lenoard Tose [the owner of the Eagles], and told him about these rooms," Jimmy recalls, "thinking fifty thousand dollars would be a good goal, and he comes back to me, generous man that he is, with, 'Well, how much for the whole floor?' I told him one million dollars, and he said, 'Well, we'll pledge that, and Jimmy, you'll get it.' "

A tall order, but then you haven't met Jimmy Murray. Eagles Fly for Leukemia had already run a few successful fashion shows with some of the players' wives, raising about $9,000 each time around. But Jimmy needed to raise more money, big money, and he needed to raise it fast. The first order of business was what turned out to be an ill-conceived radiothon, sort of a telethon of the airwaves. "I was so naive, I had the thing broken down into four quarters," he recalls. "But you just can't raise money on radio, it doesn't work. We even had WCAU-TV, the local CBS station in Philadelphia, put up our phone number for pledges during the Eagles-49ers game that day, but by the time they flashed the number we were losing something like twenty-nine to 0, and all we got were obscene phone calls. By the end of the whole thing, even with the new math, we'd only raised about eighteen dollars."

So it was back to a blank yellow legal pad to dream up another fund-raising notion, and within a month Jimmy had organized a $1,000-a-plate dinner and fashion show at the Stadium Club, where guests (mostly friends of Eagles owner

Mr. Tose) ponied up some $80,000, bringing the total monies raised by Eagles Fly for Leukemia to about $125,000. Other funds came in over the next few months, with the help of several local organizations, and when Jimmy finally turned over a check to the hospital, the doctor on the receiving end looked at him and said, "Thanks. Now, do you know what else we need?"

"We had tapped into something where so much was needed," Jimmy says, "and we were barely able to make a dent in it." What was needed this time around was a sort of halfway house, across the street from the hospital, where parents and families could stay after visiting their children, where they could take a shower or a nap or just have a cup of coffee away from the sometimes cold and impersonal hospital environment. "It was devastating to me, the impact on families faced with a child's catastrophic disease," he explains. "The divorce rate goes up to something like 70 percent under those kinds of circumstances, the entire family structure crumbles. The situation is hard enough without all the external pressures of getting by in any kind of day-to-day sense, and we thought it was important to eliminate as much of the external pressures as possible."

Eagles Fly for Leukemia was suddenly faced with a new challenge, but Jimmy was still several bricks shy of his goal. "That's when it came to me to call McDonald's," Jimmy says. "Through the Eagles I'd been dealing closely with, I don't know, between twenty-five and seventy-five corporations in the area, but for some reason something just directed me to the local McDonald's account." It was, to hear Jimmy tell it, an epiphany of sorts.

With the help of McDonald's regional director Ed Rensi (who is now the president of the company, by the way), Jimmy convened a meeting of McDonald's franchise owners in the Delaware Valley, seeking their participation in the drive. "I asked them, 'What's your next promotion? Let us be a part of it,'" he remembers. "And St. Patrick's Day was coming up, and their next promotion was their Shamrock Shakes. We asked them to pledge twenty-five cents for each shake sold, but they came back to us with an even better idea. They said they'd pledge all their money from the shakes if we'd call it the Ronald McDonald House. Gosh, we'd call it anything they wanted, just to get the thing off the ground, but as it turns out, it was probably the best-possible name for the project."

The first Ronald McDonald House was opened at 4032 Spruce Street, near the University of Pennsylvania campus, on October 15, 1974. "It was one of the greatest days of my life," Jimmy says. "I think we all had the feeling that we were there at the birth of something, that a miracle was unfolding before us on that day."

The first house had seven bedrooms and was immediately put to overuse; the house was subsequently expanded to accommodate the growing number of families in need. (A few months later, Jimmy was named general manager of the Eagles, a position he would fill for the next nine years while at the same time becoming more and more involved in the Ronald McDonald House project.) A second house was opened in 1977 in the Chicago area, and for this effort Jimmy recruited the assistance of the Chicago Bears football team; with this second house, McDonald's got involved on a national level in the project, and Ronald McDonald Houses have been appearing in cities around the country ever since. Every National Football League team is involved in the program in their home communities, as are most professional franchises in other sports. If you ask me (go ahead, ask me), it's one of the most professionally run charitable efforts I've ever seen, one that makes some of the biggest differences in the lives of the people it's there to help.

"The Ronald McDonald figure just melts kids' hearts," Jimmy says, "and like I said, he's really the perfect symbol for this whole effort." But with a company like McDonald's, one that's concerned with national standards and quality control, you might think there'd be a problem managing the bottom line of such a major community project. "We thought that, too, going in, but it hasn't been that way," Jimmy says. "Each house should have its own personality, it should acclimate toward its own community. It's important to us that the houses have big, common areas, that families have a place where they can meet in a natural way and talk about things if they want to, that there's a center of the house they can gravitate to. I'm an old neighborhood guy, and what we've done is put some of that feeling back into these houses. You can't imagine the healing benefits of a simple conversation, where one father can ask another father, 'Will Johnny's hair grow back after chemotherapy?' " When you can talk to people who've been through what you're going through, I guess you can somehow see the light at the end of the tunnel.

"On paper, this is something that would never work," Jimmy muses, "but here we are, one hundred houses later, and it works beautifully. I think it's symbolic that the houses started in Philadelphia, especially when you think about the other great piece of paper that was written here. This house, and all the subsequent houses, embody the true spirit of this country, of what it stands for." He's not kidding. Whenever I join him at the dedication of a new house, there is a special magic in the air, the room is thick with emotion and with a gratitude at what this program's accomplished.

He really gets choked up when he recounts the story of the origins of the Ronald McDonald Houses, and that's because Jimmy Murray is as decent and noble and sincere as they come. He's spent most of his working life in the front offices of professional sports organizations, from minor league baseball to the National Football League, and he brings with him an athlete's drive and dedication to every task he takes on. Lately he's been doing promotion and consulting work through his own company (he helped out on that monster Michael Jackson concert tour of a few years back), but he still finds time for his wife and five beautiful children and for the families who are touched every day by his special and enduring gift.

Yet even though he deals with the personal tragedies of families almost on a daily basis, Jimmy figures he will always be moved by what he sees. "You never get used to kids dying," he says. "It's an overwhelming event. We talk in football about playing with pain, we're into that, but nowhere in the game do you see the kind of pain and suffering these kids go through. I've met some real heroes through my work with the houses, some real saints."

What a wonderful and winning reality my friend Jimmy Murray and his co-visionaries have achieved. But the story doesn't stop here. In some respects, it's still just beginning. "It won't end until there's nobody to stay at the houses," he says.

I tip my hat to everybody who played a part in the development of this beautiful project.

★ ★

"Things only work well when everybody wins."—Billie Ann Myers at a community service awards ceremony.

WITH A LITTLE HELP FROM HER FRIENDS

★ BILLIE ANN MYERS
Little Rock, Arkansas

If there's a job needs doing, don't be surprised if Billie Ann Myers volunteers for it. And if for some reason she can't swing it herself, you can bet your boots she'll find someone who can.

Billie Ann heads the Arkansas Office of Volunteerism, an agency she helped to launch and solidify under the state's Department of Human Services, and she's made a career out of helping communities in her state grow and prosper through the spirit of giving. I love what Billie Ann Myers does for a living, because it brings out something that is basic and good in all of us and puts it to basic and good use for the community. "Don't ever let anybody tell you people don't get involved," Billie Ann insists, "because they do. Most times people just do not know there's a need, they do not know how to fill a need. If they're asked to help, and if they can help, then chances are they will." She's right, you know; I am happily astonished at the overabundance of goodwill in this country, at the way folks are willing to pitch in and lend their neighbors a hand or two. Everywhere I turn, I catch the spirit of volunteerism in full flower. I see it in our apartment building in New York, I see it on and around our farm in Virginia, and I see it just about everywhere I plant myself for the night—good people are just busting out all over with the spirit of cooperation.

That's Billie Ann's job, essentially—finding people who can help and matching them with people in need. For example, through the state's Volunteer Consultants Program, Billie Ann and her staff pulled together 150 retired Arkansas professionals—engineers, architects, environmentalists, and the like—to serve as consultants to city and county governments. Together, the consultants dispense about $650,000 worth of advice and comment each year, all of it on the house, save for expenses. "Things only work well when everybody wins," Billie Ann cautions, "and in this case everybody does win. Our local governments save money for their project budgets, obviously, but the retired professionals also win. It's a chance for them to stay involved in the professions they've made their livings at, to stay active in something that's important to their community, to offer valued input on a time schedule they can afford. All we did here was to see a need, talk to some people, say, 'What do y'all think?' and get the program going. That's the nitty gritty."

One of the things I just love about Billie Ann, as you can probably guess, is that she says things like "y'all" and "nitty gritty." Another is that she started out in this thing as a volunteer herself. After years of keeping house and raising a family, Billie Ann went to the governor's office in 1979 and volunteered her services. "I wanted to see what it was like to work in government," she explains. She was brought on, at no salary, to help with the governor's scheduling on a part-time basis. When the secretary left the state's volunteer office, which was then operated as part of the governor's office, Billie Ann was summoned to fill the vacancy. She talked her best friend into sharing the position with her. "It was one of the first job-sharing setups in the state of Arkansas," Billie Ann recalls, "least as far as the state government was concerned. We split the week, and it worked out well because you always had two energies, two fresh perspectives."

After one year on the half job, Billie Ann's friend decided to move on, and Billie Ann moved into a temporary position as a special projects coordinator. When the state government made room for a new governor in 1981, Billie Ann was the only employee to survive the shuffle in the volunteer office. She was named temporary director. "It really is true what they say about a secretary taking over," Billie Ann says now, looking back, "that a secretary is the only one who knows how an office works, how to get things done. But if you'd asked me, as a housewife, if I thought in two or three years I'd have been the director of the state Office of Volunteerism, I'd have said y'all were crazy."

Y'all ain't crazy, though, because here she is, six years later, doing a job of it. "You're never too old to start a new thing," says Billie Ann, who is fifty-three. "Look at me, I took a volunteer job in government at forty-six—as a lark, really—and here I am. And volunteering is a great way to start that something new. See if you like it, learn how an office works. In any job, in any field, someone can always make use of a helping hand, except maybe in a union-strong industry where you might be seen as a scab or something. Just ask around, and you'll find somebody to put your time to good use."

The spirit of volunteerism is in Billie Ann Myers's blood, and she'd like nothing more than to administer a statewide transfusion. "Since 1608, we have learned to solve our problems in this country through volunteerism," Billie Ann reflects. "Before we had government, before we had churches, before we had a private sector, people were working together to build their communities. Today our basic philosophy is that the only way to accommodate the community good is through the 'golden triangle' concept. You've got your government, which is the public sector, you've got business, which is your private sector, and you've got volunteers, which is your nonprofit center, and all three points on that triangle have got to work together."

Billie Ann's office serves as a middleman of sorts, a matchmaker of resources and services. "We do not have to get credit for ourselves," Billie Ann says, "we can give it away. When we start a program and give it away, by that I mean letting some other agency run the show, then it gets done better. And we can stay small." But the office does get its share of credit. It gives out some of the stuff, too; it helped to launch a program of community service awards with KARK-TV, Little Rock's NBC affiliate, honoring local volunteers. We met when I came to town to help with the awards ceremonies, and I was very much taken with Billie Ann's philosophy on volunteerism. "People only volunteer when it's to their own advantage," Billie Ann admits, "and the basic to all of it is it makes you feel good. That's one of the reasons for the community service awards, we want to promote some of the good work people are doing. Maybe people will catch on."

Although she is promoting and facilitating volunteerism, Billie Ann is paid for her work; yet she puts in long and hard hours, and you might say she is underpaid for what she does. The biggest part of Billie Ann's job is spreading the good word, something she does with a heaping helping of good cheer. "There are three ways you can get interested in volunteering," Billie Ann says. "You can inherit it, you can be taught it, or you can catch it. [The interest runs rampant through her family—her two daughters and her husband, Dub, all donate their time to one program or another.] But if you don't have the spunk yourself, you can't give it to somebody else."

She's got the spunk, Billie Ann Myers. Just listen: "It's part of our American heritage, volunteering. I believe the difference between this democracy and all of the other experiments in democracy is the willingness of the citizens of this country to stay involved. Volunteerism is the difference between us and everything else. That old saw that working women have cut into volunteerism is just not true. It's changed the patterns of volunteering in this country, definitely, but volunteerism is still alive and well. Believe me."

A lot of times, Billie Ann says, people volunteer without knowing it. "Any woman who has stayed home and raised a family has probably done a good deal of volunteer work," she says, "what with PTA meetings, carpools, coaching little league, and the like. And a lot of times people don't volunteer because they don't know how. Your yuppiest yuppie can be recruited to do something," she predicts, "and he will come through. All you have to do is ask. Maybe it'll have to be at his convenience, but that's okay. There is nothing to say it has to be painful."

So, what do you say, can we see some volunteers?

★ ★

JUST SAY NO!

★ **RUBY FERRELL CALLAWAY**
Atlanta, Georgia

Ruby Ferrell Callaway is a true national treasure. This spirited lady has turned on a very deep personal tragedy to build a grass-roots youth-awareness campaign on the perils of drug and alcohol abuse. There is no finer calling, I don't think, than to work to stop the widespread drug abuse among our children.

The thing about Ruby is that she's making a difference with a selfless vitality that has earned her a dozen major community service awards in the past year. "The awards, I don't quite know how to feel about the awards," she says softly. There is a beautiful lilt to her voice, a sincerity, the way there is with many folks from the deep South. Her sentences turn up at the end to form a question. Even her name, when it comes from her lips, sounds like poetry. "I appreciate the stroking, I think we all enjoy that. But the awards kinda bother me. I think they take a little bit away from what

Ruby Ferrell Callaway spreading the good word with her grandson.

we're actually doing in the community. You have to appreciate that the rewards and awards are two different things.
We're starting to make a difference, and that's what's important."

Nevertheless, it took one such award to help us cross paths.
Ruby was honored by WXIA-TV, the NBC affiliate in Atlanta,
in that station's community service program. Like it or not,
Ruby deserves the special attention. She has done some
wonderful work in the Atlanta area, and most of it has inspired similar doings throughout the country. A lot of what
you see in the fight against drugs and alcohol among kids
bears Ruby's imprint. It was Ruby's idea to turn Nancy Reagan's "Just Say No!" campaign into an organized walk for
area young people and their families, and before she had a
chance to take the Atlanta walk to the streets of her home
city, more than forty other communities around the country
heard about the idea and jumped on the bandwagon. By the
time the second annual walk rolled around, in May 1986,
organizers in some three hundred cities kicked up their heels
for the event. "We don't raise money," Ruby says in explaining the impact of the walks, "we raise awareness."

Awareness is important to Ruby, because it is a profound lack of awareness that took her husband away from her after twenty-five turbulent years of marriage. Her husband, her marriage, and her family were ravaged by drink. "My husband was an alcoholic," Ruby recalls now in that same sweet voice. "His disease, and what we struggled with, took a lot away from my life, and it took a lot away from the lives of my children. I remember thinking at the time that I had no personal life outside of his alcoholism, that there was no joy or happiness." There wasn't even a bearable status quo, to hear Ruby tell it: "I was coping all of the time."

Yet Ruby could not find someone to help her cope, most of all because she couldn't find someone to help her husband. "He was a good man," she says. "He deserved to be saved from this disease." But Ruby's efforts to save him fell mostly on deaf ears. Her husband, Thomas Callaway, was medically discharged from the Air Force as a schizophrenic, yet when Ruby sought treatment from the VA hospitals in her area, she was repeatedly turned away. "I used to think it was because of my color," says Ruby, who is black, "but then I realized it was not a prejudice toward me as much as it was a prejudice toward alcoholism. You have to remember, these were the times [in the late 1960s] when alcoholism was swept under the rug. People wouldn't help us because they'd say, 'No, your husband drinks, and if we help him, he'll just drink again.' That was the attitude. Everything was negative."

But Ruby's situation at home continued to deteriorate. Her husband was in and out of minor treatment and detox programs, and when he was home he was unmanageable. "He was so full of whiskey he became a diabetic," she says, "and he came down with all of the physical ills we now associate with alcoholism." On top of his illness, he was abusive, physically and mentally. During this time, Ruby says it was not uncommon for one of the couple's five children to have company over to the house, only to find their daddy lying on the floor in the living room in his shorts, passed out from drink. "My children didn't suffer for material things, but they could feel the pain," she says.

"I didn't have anybody to turn to, there was no place to go. I couldn't put him out. If I wanted to, I should've done it when he was more able to handle himself. I had to make up my mind to stay with him or to leave, and I chose to stay. I didn't know it at the time, but it was the lesser of two evils."

Her work in drug and alcohol awareness for young people is a direct outgrowth of her struggle within her own family. Ruby's husband passed on in 1974, and ever since she's dedicated herself to wiping out alcoholism and drug abuse and our ignorance about the two diseases. "When my husband died, I was angry," she says, "and in a way I guess you could say I'm doing what I'm doing for him. He was a good man, my husband, and I know if he could see me, he'd be saying, 'Do it, Ruby. Well done.' It's become almost like a mission for me."

Ruby's mission started when she decided to tell her husband's story—to local AA groups, to local councils on drug and alcohol abuse, to anyone who might listen and be in a position to help others. She was invited to speak at Peachford Hospital, a local addiction hospital where she has gone on to serve on the board for the past thirteen years. In 1978, she was appointed by the governor to serve on a state advisory council on drug and alcohol abuse, an appointment she carried out proudly for five years. "But then I finally thought, Enough of dealing with agencies and councils," Ruby states. "I started noticing that nothing was happening in the community. Nothing was happening on a grass-roots level, and I thought maybe it had to start with me."

And so, God bless her, she started organizing in the churches and schools. She helped start a group called CAS-CADE—Comprehensive Auxiliary for Southeast Communities on Alcohol and Drug Education—with a focus on youth prevention. Nancy Reagan heard about Ruby's group in April 1982, and the First Lady met with twenty-six young CAS-CADE participants during a visit to Georgia State University. "After her visit, we were really, really busy," Ruby recalls. "Before that we couldn't get any sort of grants or funding, we were the only black grass-roots group in the state, probably in the country, but after the attention from the White House, we received money for special projects."

Ruby has become something of a teen watchdog in the Atlanta area, and I think we could all serve our neighbors

191

well by following her lead in our own hometowns. Lately, Ruby has been looking to launch another annual "event" to serve as a companion to her successful "Just Say No!" walks, and what she's come up with is something she's calling a "lock-in." "We find a gymnasium or a church or some large community space, and we get the kids in to spend the night," she says. "We call it a lock-in to assure the parents that the kids won't be going anywhere outside the building and to tell the kids that they're with us for the duration. They've got to go the distance."

At the first lock-in, held in November 1986, 650 Atlanta youths were treated to an all-night program of music, martial arts demonstrations and speeches, with the general theme of the evening centered on the problems of drug and alcohol abuse. "We're finding that kids pay more attention outside the classroom setting," Ruby says, "and the lock-ins will be successful because kids will listen when they don't have to. We sent out a lot of good messages that night." Already, Ruby says, she has been flooded with calls seeking advice and comment on programs for future lock-ins in other cities.

The most astonishing thing about Ruby Ferrell Callaway, who is fifty-five, is that she does all of this in her free time, all of it from her kitchen table. "It's funny, in a way," she says, "that here we are, a nationally recognized organization, doing things that are picked up in other communities, and our headquarters are in my home. It's a real grass-roots organization." Ruby works at nights—she's a licensed practical nurse—which helps her keep her days free for her tireless organizing. "I tell people I sleep at the red lights," Ruby says when I ask her how she manages such a busy schedule. "It's a joke, but sometimes, when I'm driving to or from work, that's the only time I've got to myself. That's the only time I'm not busy."

WHEN you give a little, you get a lot, I always say. When you give a lot, like the folks you've met here, well, then you can just imagine what comes of it.

One of my deepest regrets about my current work schedule

is that it keeps me from getting knee-deep involved in some things that really matter to me and to my community. Oh, sure, I spend bunches of time at telethons and dinners and other fund-raising efforts, but my involvement tends to be more in the form of showing up and lending my name to a good cause. Now, I'm smart enough (and also immodest enough) to know that a celebrity name can sometimes lend more to a campaign than anything else I'd be able to contribute, but I do once in a while wish I could work anonymously, from the ground up, toward some noble goal. Making a speech is easy (you just write the darn thing once and have at it over and over again), but doing what Sister Kathleen Clark, Jim Murray, Billie Ann Myers, and Ruby Ferrell Callaway have done is something else entirely. They richly deserve every accolade they've received, and then some. This, hopefully, adds a little bit to the "and then some."

I'm all for "international flavor" in life.

11 The Melting Pot

WE live in a land of golden opportunity, and I want to take this opportunity to celebrate those who've journeyed to our shores to make the most of what this great country of ours has to offer.

I've always thought that it is through the eyes of an immigrant that we can best appreciate the wonders and riches of these United States. It sounds corny, but if you think about it, you'll agree. Nothing looks quite as special as it does when seen for the first time, and I've got to think an initial dose of this nation would spur some kind of love affair at first sight. My roots are purely American (I'm what you might call a red-white-and-blue-blood), so if I'm to hold to my own theory, my perspective isn't worth spit.

My folks have been here a good long while. I come from a long line of North Carolina dirt farmers on both sides of the family; we've traced my mother's father's family, the Phillipses, all the way back to the early 1700s, when they brought their mostly English and Scotch-Irish blood with them to settle here. They were farmers, all of them, and probably there was little difference in the way of life from one generation to the next. I'm not saying their lives weren't hard—believe me, my ancestors knew some hard, hard times—but there had to be a certain stability in the way they worked and lived over the years, and I can't help but think that stability was a quiet comfort whenever Lady Luck ran sour on them.

Not so for the brave and forward-thinking souls who pack up their families to seek a better life here, leaving behind everything they know and love in the process. It was true during the great wave of immigration throughout the first half of this century, and it is still true today. In many ways, the lot of our more recent immigrants has been much harder than any my family had ever known. They had to start from scratch. They came to this country, many of them, without knowing a soul, without a single marketable or translatable skill, without even the simplest command of the language. Stability wasn't even in their vocabulary, let alone in their life-style. Hard times then are not forgotten, as the old song goes.

The wave of immigration has slowed somewhat over the past few years, but they're still coming. This country—the big lug—continues to embrace the tired, the hungry, and the poor, from near and from far, and I for one am damn glad to have them, all of them. Who knows, maybe two hundred years from now the descendents of today's immigrants will talk about how their roots are purely American, about how they go back so far in this country that they've become about as native American as you can get, about how for generations their family has taken the American way of life for granted.

For now, say hello to these good people, and look through their eyes at the red, white, and blue.

★ ★

HOME COOKING

★ ROCCO MANNIELLO
Whitestone, New York

Rocco Manniello makes a lasagna that is some kind of wonderful, a chicken francese that is simply to die for (or TDF, as they say), and a fettucini that will slither its way into your heart of hearts. You can float into his restaurant on the aromas alone, like something out of a cartoon. His food is that good; it must be, to lift a hunk of apple pie like me off the ground on the smell alone.

So what's the big deal? You probably know a couple of neighborhood joints that serve up a bit of old Italy in your own hometown, probably you can cook up your own mouthwatering batch of pasta, so what makes this Rocco Manniello special? Well, what makes Rocco a special big deal to me is his place of business. He has set up a find of a restaurant in the Marine Air Terminal at New York's La Guardia Airport, a breath away from Pan Am's new Boston-New York-Washington shuttle terminal, and for a frequent and weary traveler like myself, his place is like an oasis. Really, I have to pinch myself to make sure I haven't stumbled into some sort of mirage.

Rocco's cooking is something else, but then so are a lot of things about him. When he was ten years old, he emigrated to this country with his family from Avellino, Italy, none of them knowing a word of English. They settled in the New York City borough of Queens, not far from other relatives and not far from La Guardia, and Rocco immediately set about his assimilation.

The language came fast, and so did the development of his personal work ethic; within a few years he had his own newspaper delivery route and was working part-time in more than a few neighborhood pizzerias. At fourteen, he continued his ground-up education in the restaurant business, washing tables for eight dollars a day in his uncle's Manhattan cafeteria.

"If you have ambitions, you can do anything," Rocco says over a hot plate of what he does best. Like most restaurant proprietors I know, Rocco looks like he might be his best customer; he's short and sturdy and round-looking, with just enough hair on top to make a bald-headed fellow like me a little bit jealous, but he doesn't look overweight. Hard work keeps him in shape, and it keeps him moving in the right direction. "If you work hard," he says, "and if you work toward something, then I don't care what it is, you'll do well."

Oh, has Rocco done well. When he was nineteen, he borrowed $15,000 and opened his own pizza parlor; that same year he married a former childhood classmate, after the two remet in Switzerland. (They now have two small children.) And even after he opened his first restaurant, he worked in the airport as a baggage handler for Allegheny Airlines. He's never been the kind of guy who's afraid of a little hard work, and in his case the hard work has more than paid off. It was his firsthand experience as an airport employee that got him thinking about the care and feeding of his former colleagues. "I'd do a big takeout business with the airport workers at my restaurant," he says, "something, I don't know, a few hundred lunch orders a day."

But always in the back of his mind, Rocco thought airport personnel, and his bottom line, could be better served. Workers were unable to drive airport vehicles off airport grounds, which made in-person visits to Rocco's difficult, if not nearly impossible. "Why shouldn't they be able to sit down at a nice place, a clean place with good food, quality food, at reasonable prices, and enjoy a nice lunch hour?" Rocco remembers wondering. "Why shouldn't it be easy for them to get to me, and for me to serve them?" Every successful entrepreneur I've ever met has the ability to spot a need or a hole in the marketplace; Rocco spotted his hole, and, God bless him, he filled it with mouth-watering homemade ricotta cheese.

In 1982, Rocco decided to move his talents onto airport grounds, paying $10,000 for a restaurant location that had been vacant for two years. (His other restaurant has stayed open for the nonairport crowd.) "You have to remember that, at the time, this was a very quiet terminal," Rocco says.

(You'll let old Willard put on his professor's cap for a bit of history here: the Marine Air Terminal was the original shell of what we now know as La Guardia, although almost all commercial airline business has since moved to other terminals; private and corporate jets still come in and out of the terminal, which is situated at the westernmost corner of the airport.) "All we had at the time in terms of commercial airlines was Air New England," Rocco says, putting things in perspective. "They'd fly people up to Cape Cod and back, and there wasn't a lot of carryover business from that. The only way to make money with a location like that is to cater directly to the airport workers."

And cater to them he did. There are a lot of places to eat in an airport the size of La Guardia, but most of them serve up institutionalized, processed food, the kind you might expect from a can. I've been held over and hungry in many an airport in my day, and it gives me heartburn just to think about some of the cafeteria-style food I've eaten over the years. In most airports I can't even find a good cup of coffee. Nowhere in my extensive travels have I come across the good, hearty home cooking I'm treated to at Rocco's. His manicotti and tortellini are out of this world, his stuffed shells are rich little treasures to be savored; my favorite is his baked ziti, which is almost worth the trip to New York by itself. I look at the wonderful spread he puts out, everything made fresh every day, and I think what a shame it is to serve good food like that on paper plates. "Soon I'll have real silverware and china in here," Rocco promises when I share this thought with him. "Soon."

If he says so, he will. Already he's made more than $100,000 worth of improvements on the original place, including a Port Authority–backed expansion to accommodate the arrival of Pan Am shuttle business to the terminal. The restaurant, which is formally known as the La Guardia Airport Yankee Clipper Deli Restaurant but goes by the nickname of "Rocco's," is a clean, well-lighted place. It's bright and sunny, with two walls of windows looking out onto the tarmac. You can sit there and sip some wine, or some espresso, and watch the small planes come and go or watch the airport vehicles taxi about their business; it's the nicest place

I know to pass an hour or so between flights or during a delay. The trickle-down success from Pan Am's new shuttle was slow to materialize, but as commuters became aware of his restaurant, his expanded business got off the ground. Now he serves some 1,500 customers a day, from breakfast at 6:00 each morning, to dinner at 9:30 each night.

The secret of his success, Rocco says, is in keeping the restaurant in the family. He does most of the cooking himself, and he is joined in the kitchen by his wife, his mother, and his brother. His staff is peopled with cousins and uncles and childhood friends and with workers from his other restaurant. Sometimes his grandfather, who is eighty, strolls over to the airport and cooks up a dish or two in the afternoons, just to have something to do to keep himself busy. "I don't ever want to lose that family feeling," Rocco says, "the feeling that everything here is homemade."

His wonderful recipes were for the most part picked up in his mother's kitchen, and they're assisted by his unstinting thirst for quality. "As long as you're buying quality products, you can't really make a mistake in the recipe," he says. "The quality makes up for the mistakes. It's when you skimp on things like cheeses and meats and pasta and seasonings that you don't have room for mistakes." A recipe, in other words, is only as good as the ingredients you put into it. Here are the ingredients for his mother's extra-light tomato sauce: imported plump tomatoes, fresh onions, and a light sprinkling of olive and vegetable oils. "From time to time I'll add a pork or beef bone for flavoring," Rocco admits. "The secret, though, is not to cook it for too long. A lot of times people think they need to put up a big pot of Italian sauce for hours and hours, but for this, only thirty-five minutes. That's all. After the flame is off I sprinkle fresh parsley and fresh garlic." Of course, Rocco adds his own special something he's not telling us about, and that's his own tender loving care, his own taste and feeling, his pride in a job well done.

"Look," he says, "any idiot can open a restaurant in an airport and make money. But I'm proud of my cooking, of who I am and what I do. When I see somebody enjoying something I cooked, I can't tell you how good that feels. They don't leave nothing on their plates here, no matter how big I make the portions, and that makes me feel good." He points to a clean plate on the table next to ours. "You see?" he says, reaching for the plate. "You see what I mean?

"I try my best in everything I do. I work hard here, there's a lot of sweat goes into a business like this, but it's the American dream. I had nothing when I came here, but you can do anything in this country with a little bit of ambition and dedication. I've done well, but I've had to work to do it. A lot of my friends and family, they don't work the long hours I work. A lot of them take their two or three weeks of vacation, I don't. I'm here sometimes seven days a week, sometimes fourteen, fifteen hours a day. This is not a country where you can do your job, get paid, and go home and that's it. That you can do in your own country. Here, it just doesn't stop with that. You've got to do more."

Rocco's been doing more for twenty-two years in this country. And this hungry commuter, who travels regularly between an office in New York and a home in the suburbs of Washington, can't wait to see what he serves up next.

★ ★

FROM QUINHON WITH LOVE
★ HUNG NGUYEN
Seattle, Washington

Hung Nguyen and his family—his parents, four brothers, and four sisters—fled their home in the South Vietnamese city of Quinhon just one day before the city of Saigon fell to the North Vietnamese Communists. "We just had to get out of there," recalls Hung, whose father worked for the South Vietnamese government in a position that threatened his family's future under the new Communist regime. "We could not know what would happen to us if we stayed," he says.

In April 1975, hasty arrangements were made for the trip

to the continental United States via Guam, but because of the size of Hung's family, they were separated into two groups. "Some of us came here to Seattle, and the rest of us went to Fort Wayne, Indiana," Hung recalls. "We wanted to stay all of us together, but we could not." After two years in Fort Wayne (where the winters, Hung says, were too cold, the summers too hot), the family re-formed in the Pacific Northwest, attempting to settle as a unit in their Seattle neighborhood, a community that boasts a large Vietnamese population.

Now, eleven years later, Hung's family has scattered across the country, and this, he says, is one of his greatest regrets about the way we work and live in this part of the world. "At home, the family stays much more together than here in America," he explains. "Perhaps that is the biggest difference in the culture. All of us are sad about that, but we have gotten used to it. The family unit is very much stronger where we come from, and here people in families move across the country, very far away, for school or for jobs, all of the time."

Hung lives now in an apartment with his Vietnamese wife and their American-born son, Kevin, who is two years old. His parents and some of his brothers and sisters live within several miles of his home, but it is not the same, he says, as living all of them under one roof or in one community. "Also, everything here is so expensive," Hung says. "You would not say a family like mine, with four brothers and four sisters, is so large in South Vietnam, but here in America it is much too large. It is much too expensive here for a family like that. I don't think that we can afford to have more than two or maybe three children."

I met Hung through the NBC affiliate station in Seattle— KING-TV—where he works as a graphics designer. He designs print advertising and on-air graphics, and he's got quite a flair for the job. Really, he has a special talent, and he's been able to use that talent to carve a successful and profitable career for himself. "I am more like a designer, a commercial designer, than an artist," he explains, although he paints watercolors as a hobby and teaches art at a local YMCA. "This is not a job I could have in Vietnam," he admits. "There are no television stations there like we have here, no place for me to do my job. Probably if the situation had been different and we had stayed, I would have worked for the government."

It was difficult, Hung now says, to leave his homeland without knowing if he'd ever be allowed to return, without knowing what kind of life would await him on the other side of his exodus. "I was young then," says Hung, who is now twenty-eight, "and I did not know enough to know what was happening politically, to know the meaning of everything. I just knew that my family had to leave."

In the resulting separation, Hung found himself with his parents in Fort Wayne. "When I first got here it was very difficult for me in terms of communication," says Hung. "I had studied English for many years in school at home, but when I got here it was very difficult for me. It is a difficult language, and I am still learning it."

After talking with him and with some of his colleagues, I was impressed with how naturally he has adjusted to his new culture. His English, although broken in parts, is in no need of fixing; he doesn't miss a thing when you talk with him. He has embraced his new culture with a big, broad bear hug. "I've even been to Disneyland," Hung says proudly, "although maybe I am a little bit too old for Mickey Mouse." He roots, roots, roots for his home teams—the Seattle Seahawks and Supersonics—and stops in for a McDonald's hamburger more often than he cares to admit.

Hung tells me he drives his wife crazy with his newfound passion for American food. "That's her only complaint," he says, "that I like so much the spaghetti and meat balls, the meat loaf, the hot dogs, the potato chips. I like the very simple, very quick American food. Fast food, easy to prepare. Sandwiches. For a big dinner, a big Vietnamese-style dinner, my wife has to spend two or three hours in the kitchen preparing. After that I have to spend thirty or forty minutes to do the dishes." He laughs as he says this, and I get the impression he is first realizing that his household has been truly Americanized in the space of a few years, that with his line about the dishes he has become like the stereotypical American husband. He agrees: "I would say that I have become more like the people here than I thought," he adds, "because now I like things so much to be fast and easy."

Hung is deeply proud of his American citizenship, which he won four years ago after seven years in this country. "It was a very special day for me," he says. "I felt all of the time like I owed a big deal to the people of this country, everybody was so helpful to me, and I felt that maybe by becoming a citizen I was returning something to them. I was becoming more a part of their community." Hung, like nearly every other born-again American I've met, takes his citizenship seriously; I'll even bet you he knows more about our history than I do, and that's saying something because I'm a buff for that sort of stuff. He's a good neighbor, a good friend, and an asset to his community. Probably you've noticed in your own hometown someone like Hung and his family, who make the extra effort to fit in, and the community is no doubt the better for it.

"I consider Seattle my hometown," Hung says. "It's where I live, it's where my friends and my family live, and it's been a very good place to me. Sometimes, yes, I think about maybe moving to another city or state, but it would have to be for a better job, and it would be hard to leave Seattle. This is my home."

Of course, Hung and his family would love it if they could return to their native South Vietnam, but he realizes that will likely not be possible in the near future, even for a short visit. Nevertheless, his ties to his homeland run deep; both English and Vietnamese are spoken in his home, so that his family remembers its roots. "But probably I would like to raise my son here in America," Hung admits, "even if we could go back. My son, he is an American, he was born here, and I would like him to grow up with all of the freedoms of this country. Our other children, too, when we have other children. We are Americans now, and this is where we want to raise our family."

I ORIGINALLY planned to include a visit with a charming Soviet Jewish couple who now live in St. Louis, after arriving nearly ten years ago with little more than two suitcases and the Russian equivalent of two hundred dollars to their name. I met them through some mutual friends in the area, and I was instantly taken by what they've been through. Their comments about life in America made me sit back and think about the differences between our two countries, our two peoples, and I was all excited at the chance to introduce you to them here.

But it was not to be. As we got close to publication, I got a letter from them expressing concern that their participation here might cause them headaches later on, if they ever hoped to return to Russia to visit their family. They were sorry, they said, but they felt they couldn't be included here without jeopardizing any future contact with their family back home.

I'm sorry, too, but I respect their decision, and I understand their hesitation. I regret only that we'll miss out on some of the sharp, savvy insight offered by this courageous couple, by the woman especially, since her English was a touch better than her husband's. "In Russia," she told me, "if you're an engineer, you'll die with that. Here, you try, a million things you try. You can be anything you want. And here we have friends. We didn't know anybody when we came here, and now I would say eighty percent of our happiness is our friends, and our friends are mostly Americans. If you put me in the same state, the same St. Louis, without the friends, I would feel miserable."

She also said this: "America takes time. At first I thought the people were insincere, not friendly. Why do they smile all the time? I used to think. It's so artificial, superficial. Everywhere I go, people would smile. Not so in Russia. I think, Who push them to do that? Who told them to smile? For what purpose? But then somebody told me that is just American way of looking at things. Which is better, they say, to smile or not to smile? Of course, it's better to smile. Now I walk around, I'm smiling all the time. It's a very contagious culture."

I'm glad to hear it's catching.

I've rubbed elbows with some pretty high-powered politicians in my day, as you can see from this White House photo.

12 Hail to the Chiefs

Ain't nothing quite like local politics. Really, to get a sense of how this country works, from the bottom up, you've got to get to know a few small-town politicians. They tend to be down-to-earth folks because they're cut from the salt of the earth. Oh, I've rubbed elbows with my share of high-powered governors and senators and congressmen in my day— I've even crossed paths with a president or three—but I'd sooner sit down to table with a local mayor than just about any other elected official. For some reason, higher office seems to sap the small town from the picture, and that's not a good thing. Mayors still got some small town in 'em, and that suits me just fine.

Whenever I travel with the "Today" show or on some promotional or personal appearance business of my own, I'm
usually glad-handed to death by dozens of local politicians.
Members of area chambers of commerce, city council people,
and ward officials turn out in swelling numbers for our remote broadcasts, probably on the off chance they'll land their
sincere and smiling mugs on national television. Don't get
me wrong, I kind of like all the attention (I think the folks
who say they don't are full of you know what), and most of
the winers and diners are genuinely thrilled to have a crew
from NBC News in their area. But many is the time I've
stepped aside from the maddening crowd and shared a quiet,
reflective moment with the city's top dawg.

Mayors know the mood and heart of their community better than anyone else; they wear their hometown on their
sleeve, and the longer they've been in office, well, then the
longer the sleeve, I suppose. Seriously, if you want to know
how a city's schools are faring in the wake of Reagan administration budget cuts, if you want to know how a community
has responded to a proposal to build a new, high-gloss convention center, or if you just want to know where to plant
yourself for a good, hot cup of coffee and a decent hunk of
pie, the mayor's the person to ask.

From Baltimore to Cleveland to Indianapolis, I've come to
know and admire more mayors than you could ever hope to
elect in a lifetime. I wish I could include a bit on each and
every one of them here, but in the interests of space, and in
keeping with the general neighborly tone of this book, I've
decided to visit with some of the good people at the helm of
a few of our mid-sized cities—Bismarck, North Dakota; Toledo, Ohio; Buffalo, New York; and Erie, Pennsylvania. I've
spent some special time with each of them, and I've been
bowled over by the lot of them.

To know a town, you've got to know its mayor. Get to know
these four, and you'll have a pretty good picture of what life
is like in their part of my neighborhood.

Bus Leary knows Bismarck like the back of his hand.

A FULL-TIME MAYOR ON A PART-TIME SALARY

★ BUS LEARY

Bismarck, North Dakota

The first time I met Bus Leary he turned out in an old-fashioned stagecoach to pick me up at the local airport. No kidding. There he was—no less than the mayor of the fair city of Bismarck, North Dakota—with four head of horses and a fancy old carriage and the biggest, proudest smile I'd seen in quite some time. I've flown into a lot of airports in my day, and I've been greeted by more dignitaries than you'd care to see in one place at one time, but I've never been made to feel welcome so quickly as I was in the kind hands and warm heart of Bus Leary.

After a start like that, Bus and I hit it off just fine. (By the way, the stagecoach was paid for by the Bismarck Convention Tourist Bureau, an indication, presumably, of the down-to-earthiness of the Bismarck people.) I was in town to speak at the North Dakota Education Association state convention, and Bus went out of his way to see I was well taken care of. He didn't have to work too hard.

Bus Leary knows Bismarck like the back of his hand. He should; he's lived there for more than fifty years. It's a pretty place, Bismarck and surrounding parts, nestled out there in the Red River valley, not far from the vast open spaces known as the Badlands. The whole area is an important part of the American landscape, and you can't help but marvel at the spirit of the people and the lay of the land when your tour bus is a stagecoach and your tour guide is an enthusiastic native like Bus. He arrived in town as a teenager (he had grown up in the southwest corner of the state), with a twenty-dollar bill and not much else to his name. "My father took me aside one day, gave me the money, and said, 'Time for you to go and find a job,'" Bus recalls. "So I just made my way up to Bismarck and took the first thing that came along."

The first thing that came along was a job as a stock boy in a local grocery store; there must have been something about all that fruit and produce and meat and dry goods because Bus stayed in the grocery business for the next thirty some odd years. Before his retirement at the age of fifty-five, Bus owned and operated two downtown Super Value supermarkets. "I worked my way up from the low end," he says.

But retirement didn't come easy for Bus—he was restless and bored and desperate for something to devote his full energies to—and when he wasn't satisfied with the five declared candidates for mayor one election year, he decided to toss his hat into the ring as well. "I felt I owed the city something," he recalls. "The city was good to me, the people supported me and my stores, and I thought it was my turn to do something for the good people here. I never thought about it like I was in politics or anything. In North Dakota you don't have to declare your party ties, which is good because I don't have any party ties. I'm not really a party man. I'm kind of a person man. I thought I'd be a good leader, I thought I'd be able to get things done."

You've got to love the way Bus went about his campaign. He'd stop people on the street to see what was on their minds, or sometimes he'd even canvas support door to door. Most people already knew him from his days at the grocery store or from his involvement with the local chamber of commerce, but he didn't leave anything to chance. To hear him tell it, the campaign sounds like something you'd sooner find in a small-town election, but Bismarck is the biggest city for over two hundred miles in that part of the country.

"I campaigned on the fact that I'd be a full-time mayor on a part-time salary," Bus remembers. "I think that's what did it for me, that's what set me apart from the pack. I didn't care about the money, and I didn't have anything else to do during the day, so why not promise to work full-time?" When Bus was vying for the position, the mayor of Bismarck earned a monthly salary of $250.

Bus, as you've probably guessed by now, won that election, and when he took office he attacked the position with such dedication that the monthly salary worked out to little more than a dollar an hour. "I was in my office every day from eight in the morning to five in the afternoon," he says proudly, "and of course there were some evenings and weekends where I was needed at a function or event, but I enjoyed every minute of it. People knew I was always available if they needed me, and they always knew where to find me."

By the time I first found Bus he was serving his second four-year term. (He ran unopposed as the incumbent.) The city's hospitals had almost doubled in size, the entire downtown area had been revitalized, and a big new civic center was thriving. During his tenure Bus was also instrumental in attracting a large hotel chain to what has fast become one of this country's leading convention centers. The city of Bismarck, it's fair to say, was getting far more than its money's worth from the office of the mayor.

Bus has since stepped down as mayor, and now, at seventy years old, he is finally enjoying the retirement days he'd set his sights on in the first place. "I thought it was time to give someone else a chance at the job," Bus says. "I thought I should step aside and take it easy." Of course, Bus still keeps an eagle eye on his old office; the new mayor, he says, doesn't put in nearly half the hours he managed, but Bus says that's all right with him. "Look," he reasons, "you can't fault a fellow for not working as hard at a thing as you did. As long as you put everything you can into a job, that's all you can ask. I had more time than other people, that's all. Maybe I spoiled people into thinking they deserved a full-time mayor, I don't know."

Bus takes care of the details, and he goes the extra distance in everything he does. I remember when it came time for me to leave Bismarck that first time we met, I was running late; I had to be in Chicago the next morning, and my scheduled flight was the last one out that night. But Bus saw to it that I made my plane, and then he went over to my hotel and forwarded my bags for me. You don't expect that kind of we-aim-to-please behavior from a mayor of a city the size of Bismarck; you don't expect that kind of treatment from anybody. He even found the time to make sure I left town with a homemade pecan pie.

As I was leaving, the last thing Bus said to me was, "I want to live to be one hundred, so you can mention my name on the air," referring, of course, to my current habit of congratulating this country's centenarians on their hundredth birthdays. Well, Bus, I'll be honored to do the honors then, but I thought I'd also mention your name here. After all, who knows where I'll be in thirty years?

★ ★

HOLY TOLEDO!

★ **DONNA OWENS**
Toledo, Ohio

Don't mess with Donna Owens, the housewife-turned-second-term-mayor of Toledo, Ohio. And whatever you do, don't go dragging the good name of her fair city through the Mud Hens. Donna Owens is fiercely proud of her hometown, as are most of the local folks I had a chance to meet when I visited there, and she is first in line to defend Toledo against bad raps and hard knocks.

"The only things people know about Toledo are the Mud Hens and 'M*A*S*H,' " she says, referring to the local minor

"Nobody expected I'd ever turn out to be mayor of Toledo, least of all me."
—*Donna Owens.*

league baseball team and to the popular situation comedy that featured Toledo as the hometown of one of its main characters. "I'm out to change all that."

She really is. One songwriter found himself on the wrong side of the Toledo city fence when he made the mistake of writing a not-so-favorable song, "Saturday Night in Toledo, Ohio," which appeared on a John Denver album. Leave it to Donna Owens to know how to deal with the likes of him. "We invited him back to Toledo to try and change some of his impressions," she recalls. "We made a whole big thing out of it. We even had a casket out there and buried his song in it. He came in thinking he'd get a key to the city, or something like that, but no way. Absolutely not. He wrote another song for us, which he sang when he was here, but until he records it, or until he gets someone like John Denver to record it, and until it's a hit, he's not getting a key."

But recasting the national image of her hometown is only a small part—albeit the fun part—of Donna Owens's job as the fiftieth mayor of this ethnically mixed city of more than 350,000. (In case you were wondering, Donna is the first woman ever elected to the office and the first Republican in sixteen years to win the honor in her heavily Democratic city.) The big part, and the hard part, is working to keep the

211

city back on its feet, now that she's helped the community stand up again.

Saturday nights in Toledo, Ohio, haven't always been as rosy as they are now. When Donna Owens first entered public office (she served on the city council for six years before being elected mayor in 1983), the city was slumping through a years-long sit-down. Toledo was facing its highest unemployment rate in city history, city parks were in disrepair and disarray, and garbage pickup had been reduced to every other week. As a city council member, Donna championed a payroll tax bill that called for a temporary .75 percent increase earmarked for capital improvements, general funds, and police and fire maintenance; the bill passed by a narrow margin, and the city was soon on the mend.

"In a short time you were really able to see the new tax dollars at work," Donna says with part of the fierce pride that has come to characterize her term as mayor. "We saw a dark, depressed, decayed area revitalize into a vibrant, excited community. The transformation was really incredible. Our parks looked beautiful, the city was clean, new jobs were created, we were really on a roll."

But shortly after Donna began her first mayoral term, the fiscal bottom fell out from under the city, and Toledo's roll slowed to a backward tumble. You may remember the fiasco surrounding many Ohio savings and loan institutions in 1985; if you don't, you can at least guess at the trouble awaiting Donna Owens. The city of Toledo lost $19.2 million when one of its uninsured investments went belly up. "You can't imagine the turmoil in the community," she says now. "People were after my neck."

But before her constituency could get its collective hands around her throat, Donna took the offensive: she asked for the resignations of those responsible for the mismanaged funds, and she asked the voters to continue the temporary payroll tax for another four years. She also asked them to vote for her again. "Do you realize how crazy that was?" she says, looking back. "Do you know how absurd it is to ask people to accept a new tax when we had just mismanaged over nineteen million of their tax dollars? But they accepted my proposals and gave me another chance. We passed every single tax issue that year, which is a story no other city in this country could tell.

"All of this speaks, I think, to the incredible resiliency of the people of this community. I took their vote not as a vote of confidence, and not as an endorsement, but as an indication that people here loved their city and didn't know where else to turn. It's sort of like they said to me, 'Okay, serve another term, but we'll be watching you.' "

They're still watching her, the good people of Toledo, Ohio, but now they're looking on in wide-eyed and appreciative wonder. Less than one year later, Donna Owens had seen to it that $13 million of the mismanaged funds were returned to city coffers through monies raised by the new payroll tax. She has, as we forecasters are fond of saying, weathered the storm.

For a Toledo housewife with three daughters, the notion of helming the city government is of the pie-in-the-sky variety, but for Donna Owens it is unexpected reality. "This wasn't anything like I'd planned on," she admits. The first time she got involved in local politics was when she attended school board meetings, she says, "to show concern over my children's education or what I deemed to be their lack of education." From there to here it's been a fast ride, and not an easy one, but it's a whirlwind she wouldn't trade for anything. And judging from the way the people of Toledo turned out in her support, they wouldn't trade her for anyone.

The last time I was in town, we had a chance to lock heads for a private, serious talk, and I was extremely taken by Donna's outlook: "I'm a very patriotic person," she reflects. "I believe in the American dream, and part of the American dream tells us that it's possible for anybody to be anything, to go beyond what's expected of them. Nobody expected I'd ever turn out to be mayor of Toledo, least of all me, and yet here I am. People used to tell me things like 'You're a nice lady, but you'll never get elected mayor.' I've been incredibly blessed in public life, and incredibly blessed in my private life. But this is what I mean when I talk about the American dream. This is what it's all about."

I'll buy that. In fact, I'll take two.

★ ★

"I make a lot of decisions as mayor, and if I'm right, then that's just frosting on the cake."—James D. Griffin.

SHUFFLIN' OFF TO BUFFALO

★ JAMES D. GRIFFIN
Buffalo, New York

I got off on the wrong foot with Jimmy Griffin, the three-term mayor of Buffalo, but he set things right before too long. I made the mistake of saying something not too nice about his city on national television—something about their persistent snow and cold, if I remember—and the next thing I knew my phone was ringing off the hook with demands for my head, my neck, and my job.

By way of public apology, I offered to travel to Buffalo and personally shovel the snow from the mayor's driveway, as a measure of my good faith and relative humility. (It also struck me as a good way to keep my head, my neck, and my job.) Wouldn't you know it, Jimmy Griffin took me up on my offer (I was hoping he'd let it slide), and before I could hum a few bars of "Buffalo gals, won't you come out tonight, come out tonight . . ." I was shuffled off to Buffalo (some folks would say I wasn't shuffling with a full deck) to make good on my word. You might say I was buffaloed into the situation.

Turns out I almost made the trip for nothing, and although they weren't exactly having a tropical heat wave when I hit town, there wasn't a shovelable flake of snow to be found. But Buffalo Mayor Jimmy Griffin is not the sort to leave well enough alone; he saw to it that a truckload of the man-made stuff was delivered from a nearby ski resort (Kissing Bridge). Anything to see me sweat.

So there we were, Jimmy Griffin and me, shoulder to shoulder, shoveling unnatural snow off his driveway under the most unnatural of circumstances, all of it under the watchful eye of the local media. And after an unnatural introduction like this, Jimmy Griffin and I became friends. Naturally.

As the only mayor in Buffalo history to be elected to three consecutive terms in office, Jimmy Griffin has earned a reputation as a tough, feisty, and conservative leader. He has run with the endorsements of the local Democratic, Republican, Conservative, and Right-to-Life parties, and although he is a registered Democrat, he was elected to his current term without the endorsement of his own party. "The local paper calls me a Republicrat," Jimmy confesses. "I try to represent the people more than I represent any party. The more political ties you have, the less effective you can be."

For those of you who've never been, Buffalo is a pretty city of some 340,000 residents, with a beautiful waterfront area and crisp, clean mountain air. The city, one of the leading flour-milling centers in the country, has long had the image of a blue-collar town, but that image is slowly changing. Too often, people like me give places like Buffalo a bad rap on the national weather map, and that's something Jimmy Griffin hasn't quite learned to live with over the years. "Johnny Carson," Jimmy says, "he's the biggest offender. But I can handle all of them. Whenever I hear something like that, or whenever I read something negative, I always write to the offending parties. Usually I'll invite them up for a visit, to see what a beautiful place this really is, and most times that keeps them quiet." Don't I know it.

Lately, Jimmy's biggest push for national respect has been

through the office of Major League Baseball Commissioner Peter Ueberroth. He hopes to land a professional baseball franchise for the city, and he likes his chances. "If they expand to six new teams, which appears likely, then it looks like we have a shot," he figures. To this end, ground has already been broken on a 19,500 seat open-air grass-field stadium, which will be completed in time for the 1988 baseball season; the park is designed for use by the city's triple-A minor league franchise and will be expandable, within a period of eight months, if needed, to a seating capacity of 45,000. "That's what they like to see for a major league team," Jimmy says. "They don't want another domed stadium, particularly up north where that's been the tendency in recent years. They want to see baseball played outdoors, on natural turf, and they want to be able to seat between forty and fifty thousand." Baseball officials estimate that a decision will be made on the next phase of major league expansion by 1991.

"You can't begin to guess at the impact something like that would have on this city, on the whole surrounding community," says Jimmy, whose interest in the sport stems from his days in the service, when he roamed the outfield at Fort Dix for a team led by former major league pitcher Harvey Haddix. (Haddix, for the nonfans among you, once pitched a perfect game—not allowing a single runner to reach base—for twelve innings. And lost.)

And Jimmy Griffin is not one to put his mouth where his money isn't: a few years back he led a group of forty local investors who kicked in $1,000 each to bring a double-A minor league team to the city. "We lost our shirts," Jimmy says, "but we brought organized baseball to the area. That's something."

Jimmy held his first public office at a young age (he served two terms as a district councilman, beginning at the age of thirty-two), and he lived at home with his mother during the first several years of his public life. "Why not?" he says. "You can't beat home cooking." By the time he married and moved out of the house, Jimmy was thirty-nine years old. "My wife, Marge, knew what she was getting into as far as politics was concerned," he recalls. "On our first date I took her to hear a speech." The speech, of course, was his own. (Marge Griffin, by the way, has had me over for dinner, and she makes the meanest pot roast her side of Lake Erie.)

From councilman, Jimmy moved to the New York State Senate in 1967, representing the southern portion of the city and most of southern Erie County. In 1977 he was elected mayor, and he has since succeeded in reversing the trends of a once stagnating city. When he took office, the city's waterfront area was an eyesore—it was nothing more than a swamp with empty beer cans, really—and it has since been transformed into a showcase of commercial, residential, and recreational development. He has also succeeded in spurring the redevelopment of the city's decaying downtown area, attracting a new Hyatt Regency hotel and new headquarters buildings for Goldome and Liberty-Norstar Banks. An inherited $19 million deficit was returned to the city under Jimmy's tight fiscal management after only three years, and his administration has continued to operate at a surplus throughout his tenure in office.

"I make a lot of decisions as mayor," Jimmy assesses, "and I can't be right all of the time. If I'm wrong, then hopefully I'll have a chance to correct my mistake. If I'm right, that's just frosting on the cake. But whether I'm right or wrong, the reporters here and I are always fighting or arguing over something." That sort of adversarial relationship with the press sometimes comes with a mayor's territory, but when the local newspaper gives Jimmy a hard time, he is quick to return the favor: "They don't celebrate Christmas over at the *News*," he jokes at the newspaper's expense, "because they can't find three wise men over there."

Yet despite Jimmy's prominent position in the city, he remains a good old boy, a down-to-earth fellow whose roots and beliefs run deep in the community. He still pals around with some of his cronies from his pre–public office days when he worked in the feed mills and grain elevators on the city's waterfront and as an engineer on the Buffalo Creek Railroad. "Sure, I still like to go down and have a couple of drinks with the boys," Jimmy admits, "but it's tough when you're mayor.

You can't really let your hair down, even though I don't have that much hair to let down." (I'm walking on the ground he's talking about on this one.)

But Jimmy Griffin has got more than enough hair for someone like me to stand on end when I mouth off at his city's expense. Come to think of it, I'm almost glad I tossed a semi-disparaging remark in his direction way back then. It gave us an excuse to meet, and it gave me a chance to see one of our most flamboyant local leaders work his magic on one of our most unheralded cities.

★ ★

"I may be the only mayor in this country who is listed in the phone book."—Louis J. Tullio.

BY POPULAR DEMAND

★ LOUIS J. TULLIO
Erie, Pennsylvania

When you've got a good thing going, you tend to stick with it.

The city, and people, of Erie, Pennsylvania, have got a good thing going with Louis J. Tullio, and the voters there just can't seem to get enough of a good thing. Lou is currently serving his sixth term as mayor, a post he's held for twenty-two years. That's quite an achievement; in fact, it's a record achievement in Erie politics, and as far as we can tell there's only one mayor in this country who's been in office longer— Milwaukee Mayor Henry W. Maier, who recently marked his twenty-seventh year in office.

"I've never had a free ride," Lou insists. "I never had the chance to run unopposed. There's always been someone up against me." One time, the first time, the someone up against him got the better of Lou in the Democratic primary, and it appeared his mayoral career would never get off the ground. Lou lost the nomination by three hundred votes, but his opponent and Democratic nominee died just weeks before the general election, and in the mixed-blessing aftermath the party asked Lou to run as its second choice. Lou beat the incumbent mayor in the November 1965 election and promptly earned the nickname "One Term Tullio" in the local papers. "For some reason, the people thought I'd serve one term and that would be it," he recalls. "I still got some of the O.T.T. buttons they had printed up."

Boy, were they wrong about Lou Tullio. The local media has grown somewhat kinder to him over the years, although the morning newspaper is now run by someone with a personal interest in Lou's political future. "My daughter is married to the editor," Lou says, "and sometimes that's tough on both of us. Sometimes the 'family ties' thing gets in the way of what we both have to do." Nevertheless, the paper his son-in-law edits has endorsed him during the last two elections, and in the last election he won the unanimous approval of the paper's editorial board. "I got a kick out of that one," Lou recalls. "My son-in-law was out of town at the time, and I would tell everyone I was glad he wasn't there when they voted. If he was, the endorsement probably wouldn't have been unanimous."

Erie is a good-size city with a small-town feel. It's the third-largest city in Pennsylvania (behind Philadelphia and Pittsburgh), and a center of industrial manufacturing in that part of the state. It's one of my favorite places. The city is beautifully situated on the shores of Lake Erie, and there is a booming tourism business in place there, particularly now that Lou has succeeded in attracting a Hilton hotel to the city's bay-front area. "Everybody knows everybody else around here," Lou says, "so you get the best of everything. There are museums and convention centers and theaters and good restaurants and pretty much everything you could want in a big city, but it's also very much like a small town."

Lou must be doing something right to win reelection every four years since who can remember. "I wouldn't have been elected six times if I hadn't accomplished anything," he says matter-of-factly. What he's accomplished can often be easily spotted, because much of what he's added to the Erie community has been named in his honor. An apartment complex providing housing for area senior citizens goes by the name of Tullio Towers; the city's convention center, which seats eight thousand people for all manner of events, has carried his name since it opened in 1983; and the athletic field at nearby Mercyhurst College has also been named in his honor. And the city's Presque Isle Beach area—a seven and a half mile stretch of sand jutting out into Lake Erie—is undergoing a $110 million redevelopment that, though it doesn't bear his name, clearly bears Lou's mark. "We're hoping to turn it into something like the South Street Seaport in New York or Faneuil Hall in Boston," he says. "It should be a terrific boost to the community."

One of the things I love about Lou is the no-nonsense attitude he brings to his office. He recently supported a Republican candidate for governor of Pennsylvania, despite his Democratic party ties, explaining, "I put the city ahead of politics." I like that. If one of his disgruntled constituents calls him at three in the morning to complain about something like the lack of snow or leaf removal, Lou will take care of the problem and make sure to phone back with a progress report. At three in the morning. I like that, too.

I also like the fact that his home telephone number is listed in the phone book. "I've always had my phone number in the book," Lou says. "I remember at the last mayor's conference, the subject came up. [Lou has served as a director of the Democratic Mayors of the U.S. Conference of Mayors.] I think it's important to be available to the people in your community, but everybody there thought I was crazy. I may be the only mayor of a big city in this country who lists his home phone number, but I always know the pulse of the people. I can always be reached." Lou's wife, Grace, helps him screen some of the calls, which makes Lou's open-phone policy less of a burden than it might seem.

Like Jimmy Griffin from Buffalo, Lou Tullio is a former jock. Lou used to play football at Holy Cross College in Worcester, Massachusetts. When he joined the Holy Cross squad, Lou played fullback, but he converted to the guard position to make room for a pretty fair future all-pro named Bill Osmanski, a hard-hitting fullback who went on to star for the Chicago Bears. After college, football stayed in Lou's blood, and he later returned home to coach the inaugural team at Erie's Gannon College. With Lou at the reins, Gannon fielded its first football team ever in 1949 and went on to a miraculous undefeated season. (The team was unscored upon in its first five games!) Lou was named Little All-American Coach of the Year and brought the tiny school to national attention.

He looks like a football player, my friend Lou. He's a big fellow with a big smile, and for a man of seventy he looks pretty darn good. (I wouldn't want to rumble with him, let's put it that way.) Lately, though, Lou has moved his sporting drive to the golf links, and he tries to sneak in a few rounds whenever possible. He credits his lifelong interest in sports with keeping him young in spirit, mind, and body, and I have to think he's on to something here.

Lou Tullio has come a long way in his hometown, but he for one is not surprised at his achievements. "I always used to tell my father, 'Someday I'll be the mayor of Erie,' " Lou recalls. "That's the truth. For some reason I always thought I'd wind up mayor, even as a kid. I'm only sorry my father didn't live long enough to see me make good. I've always regretted that." Lou's father died before Lou was elected to office; his mother died just last year, at the age of ninety-two, having had the unique thrill of watching her son call the shots in her hometown for almost twenty years.

If they could see him today, both parents would be proud. He's done quite a job for the city of Erie, and he continues to do so after all these years. Who knows, he just might have another six terms left in him. I wouldn't be surprised.

PERMIT me a few words on two of the heads of city not included here:

During most of my work weeks, I live in a city with perhaps the most colorful mayor in the country—New York's Mayor Ed Koch. I don't want to get into a discussion of politics and policy here (the way I tried not to in the profiles previous), but you've got to grant that Mayor Koch can be one outrageous character. He's smart, he's quick, and he says what's on his mind, no matter what the political consequences. Sometimes, as I catch his act on the local news, it seems that Koch doesn't realize his particular small town just happens to be the biggest, most exciting city in the country. He's about as down home as you can get—in some ways he's almost a hayseed in the big city—and he puts on a great show. We've bumped into each other at a few functions over the years, and I'm always wowed by the way he handles himself—with Mayor Koch, what you see is very definitely what you get.

But Ed Koch is not the only mayor to raise America's eyebrow over the past few years. I've also done a lot of work with Mayor Henry Cisneros of San Antonio, Texas, and I bet you'll be hearing more and more about him on the national level in the years ahead. He's a class act, Mayor Cisneros, a good-looking young guy who knows how to play to the cameras. Once he dressed as Santa Claus and jumped into the San Antonio River for a national television special. How can you not love a guy who'll pull a stunt like that? A man after my own heart is Mayor Cisneros. On the serious side, he's done a lot for his community, and the city of San Antonio is riding the wave of his popularity to become one of our most vibrant and important cities in the middle South. I cherish my visits there.

Some of my favorite old folks, like 104-year-old Reba Kelley, have got more energy than I do, and they've got about 50 years on me.

13 The Century Club

SOMEBODY smarter than I'll ever be once said that age is a matter of mind—if you don't mind, it doesn't matter. I am reminded of this all the time, and I am reminded of it again now as I sit down to write this. I am on the Concorde, heading across the Atlantic from London to New York. They tell me the whole trip will take just under three and a half hours, and there is a feisty old woman sitting in front of me who seems determined to keep eating and drinking for the duration. Her ticket cost her five thousand dollars, and from the way she's going it looks like the price will just about cover her food and drink.

I first noticed her back at the airport—they've got a luxurious lounge at Heathrow for Concorde passengers—and she made four trips to the complimentary buffet table they'd had set out there, then she stuffed her purse with four or five candy bars. Here, on the plane, she's already sampled everything on a roving cheese tray, and she's got a brandy set up next to her second gin and tonic. She even took a cigar from the flight attendant who offered them, and I confess I was mildly surprised when she didn't light up; instead she tucked it away in her purse, presumably for later.

I flagged down a passing stewardess. "This lady is incredible," I said. "How old is she?" I thought from the way she moved and carried herself maybe she was sixty-five, perhaps seventy; it's possible she was a terrific-looking seventy-five.

"She's ninety-three," answered the stewardess.

Ninety-three? At first I couldn't believe it. I mean, this old lady has the spirit, fight, and gumption of a woman half her age. But then I stopped to think about it, and I wasn't really surprised at all. More and more I hear incredible stories about the most senior of our country's senior citizens, and what was once disbelief on my part has turned to sheer wonder. Talk about amazing stories! Steven Spielberg could learn a thing or three from the tens of thousands of centenarians who were born long before the very idea of still pictures (let alone moving ones) had caught on in this country.

When it comes to centuries-old traditions, there are none grander than the hundreds of men and women I am lucky enough to meet and congratulate on the occasions of their one hundredth birthday. And from the looks of things, I'll have my work cut out for me in the years ahead. Centenarians are among the fastest-growing age groups in America; there are some 40,000 people in this country now over the age of one hundred, and by the year 2000 there figures to be over 100,000. People are living longer than ever before, and this alone is changing the face of many of our social systems in this country. The nuclear family is undergoing a late-in-life shift as more and more children are faced with taking care of the parents who once cared for them. And the residential facilities once designed simply for prolonged care of the elderly are now offering resident seniors a fuller, richer life than they've had to before. Of course all this puts an extra burden on taxpayers, and on our Social Security system, but this, I think, is a small price to pay for the privilege of peopling our communities with the folks who've been around long enough to help put our modern world in some kind of perspective, to help us understand where we're going by teaching us where it is we've been. For too long, old people have been this country's greatest untapped natural resource, and I for one am thrilled that the needs and triumphs of this growing group are coming to greater attention. It is through them, and only through them, that we will be able to build an effective bridge from our past to our future.

Like every good thing that's ever happened to me in my career, my involvement with senior citizens happened almost by accident. It was a fluke, really; I just kind of backwarded myself into something that would change my whole life. Here's the story. About six years ago, a friend asked me to wish his Uncle Clarence a happy one hundredth birthday on the air, the sort of request I received all the time but always had to decline because of the perceived ethics of network news. But then it occurred to me—hey, somebody is turning one hundred; if that's not newsworthy, then I don't know what is. So I went against standard practice, and against the advice of the network, and wished old Clarence good health and good wishes over the air. But there was no way to prepare for what happened next. I thought maybe I'd get the old hand slap for bucking the system, but instead what I got was a slow stream of similar requests. Actually, it started out as little more than a drip. (And if you asked some people, they'd tell you that's how I started out, too. Ba-dump-bump.) Two weeks later the drip turned to a trickle with two or three requests. I had struck a chord. Here was something —sending out birthday greetings across the miles to people who truly deserved a tip of the hat—that nobody else was doing. It was different. It was also folksy and homey and patriotic, and it fit me like a glove. And the network left me alone to do my thing. All because of Uncle Clarence, God bless him.

Now I receive as many as forty requests a day, and I try to verify and announce as many as I can; hopefully I'll get to at least one in each of my four segments every weekday morning. Those I can't mention on the air I send my good wishes to in the mail. (A note to the social scientists among you: Requests are heaviest during the months of November and December, and I suppose from that we can extrapolate some pretty interesting theories about how and when our forebears got down to business in the years leading up to the gay 1890s.)

It's fitting, I think, that someone named Clarence was the very first centenarian I celebrated on the "Today" show; Clarence, you'll remember, was the name of the angel in Frank Capra's movie *It's a Wonderful Life* (it's a wonderful movie, by the by), the angel who turned Jimmy Stewart's life around by showing him the many good things in his world that went unnoticed. My Clarence never knew it, but he was an angel, too; he changed my life. My work with old people in this country has rewarded me like nothing else I have ever done. I have visited dozens of nursing homes and retirement communities, and I am always moved by the impact I am able to make with my visits. I think I always will be. Most of the old folks I've met are caring and sensitive and desperate for affection; they're lonely, unfortunately—many of them have outlived most of their immediate family—and I like to think my reaching out to them has made a difference, has made them feel more a part of the world they live in, a world that for too long has taken them for granted.

As for the birthday greetings themselves, they've quickly become an American tradition. My office has turned into this country's unofficial clearinghouse for soon-to-be centenarians. (There is also this place in Washington called the White House, perhaps you've heard of it, where they do a fine job of identifying and congratulating one-hundred-year-olds in this country; but they've got to take care of some other business as well, and I am happily easing their burden in this area.) I'm known for my birthday greetings to the senior set more than anything else I've ever done in my thirty-five years in this business. Viewers of all ages, I think, are uplifted by my celebration of these grand old folks; there is a deep-seated respect for age in this country, a respect that cuts across all issues of race and social and economic class, and it seems I've plugged into something through which we can all draw quiet inspiration. Everywhere I go, people trot out an elderly relative they'd like me to meet. Once, when I was in Lansing, Michigan, a big yellow school bus pulled up to where we were doing our remote, and one of the kids stuck his head out the window and hollered, "Hey, Willard! Will you mention my birthday in eighty-five years?" I get reactions like this all the time, and it thrills me to see the kind of impact you can have through the power of television. It also keeps me humble.

Myron Cohen, the late great borscht belt comic, who himself lived to a ripe old age, used to tell a wonderful story about a 104-year-old man, a joke that bears repeating here. As Myron told the story, the old man stopped by his doctor's office one day for his annual checkup, and after being presented with a clean bill of health, he turned to the doctor and said, "See you next year."

"That's wonderful," said the doctor. "Not to alarm you or anything, but here you are, 104 years old, and yet you're so confident you'll be healthy for another year. Tell me, how can you be so sure?"

"It has nothing to do with confidence," replied the old man in a thick, rich Yiddish accent, an accent I could never do justice to in person, let alone on paper. "It has to do with statistics, and statistics say that between the ages of 104 and 105, not too many people die."

I love that story. Not because it's side-splittingly funny (sometimes it doesn't even register a laugh when I tell it, although that probably has more to do with my bungling attempt at a thick, rich Yiddish accent than anything else), but because it speaks to a deeper truth about age and reason, about the keen insight and rare perspective you'll find among this country's only priceless antiques.

Another old joke, and you can take "old" to mean whatever you want in this case, has it that a hundred-year-old man named Goldfarb walked into a church and sat down in the confessional. "Father," he said, "I make love every day to a twenty-five-year-old girl." The priest whispered back through the confessional: "But Mr. Goldfarb, you're Jewish. Why are you telling this to me?" To which Goldfarb replied, "Are you kidding? At my age, I'm telling everybody." This one holds nothing in the way of redeeming qualities, but I love it just the same.

There are some wonderful jokes about old folks, but the funniest stories of all just happen to be true. Oh, I've met some terrific old characters on the road, folks we'd all love to have as our own crotchety old aunt or curmudgeonly uncle. Boy, can I tell you stories! Like the time I asked a woman if in her hundred years she'd ever been bedridden, and she told me, "Oh, yes, thousands of times, and once in a buggy, but don't you dare mention that on television." (I think she rehearsed that one.) Or the time a sweet old man took me aside and confided in me that he still likes the girls, although, he said, "I can't exactly remember why." Then there's my favorite retired army colonel—Charles Norris of Charlotte, North Carolina—who told me how he can't abide the anxious stockbrokers who try to sell him on municipal bonds that won't mature for twenty years: "Hell," he said, "at my age, I don't even buy green bananas."

Somebody wrote to me once about their ninety-five-year-old aunt, who used to drink four to six ounces of gin a day, until her doctor told her she had to give up gin. She did, and now she drinks brandy. Or the ninety-two-year-old renaissance man who really, truly, is my honest-to-goodness neighbor down in Delaplane, Virginia—Eddie Strother—who lives by himself and still keeps his farm going all winter long. I ask Eddie all the time when he plans to retire, and he asks me back: "Retire to what?" His perspective on life is more than refreshing—it's vivifying; one of his favorite expressions is, "You rust out a hell of a lot quicker than you wear out." (You'll have a chance to spend a little time with Eddie a bit later in this chapter.) These are the kind of old folks I love, the ones who live their lives the way they damned please; they've made it this far, so by golly, let's leave 'em alone to keep doing what they're doing. They must be doing something right.

Recently, I ran across a good-looking older woman in Terre Haute, Indiana, the kind of woman who, even in her later years, is very vain about her appearance. She took me aside after we were introduced, looked at me shyly and girlishly, and said, "Willard, how old do you think I look?" Now if ever there was a real stumper of question, that was it. Keep in mind, this woman was 103, but I played the diplomat in the thing and told her she looked about 70, just to be on the safe side. "Oh," she said, patting her hair in obvious disappointment. "Most people say I don't look a day over sixty." Sometimes you just can't win, but in a case like this one you don't really mind losing.

Two of my favorite centenarian stories took place at the "Today" show. In the first, my celebration of the one-hundred-plus set almost backfired, and I mean literally back-fired. We brought on a lovely man from New York City, a man who went to work every day up until his hundredth birthday, and somebody got the bright idea of doing up a little birthday party after our interview. Well, this being morning television, we trotted out a cake with one hundred blazing birthday candles. Now, I don't know about you, but I'm not the sort of guy who should stand too close to one hundred blazing candles, birthday or otherwise. One candle would have served quite nicely, thank you very much. There I was, cake cradled cautiously in my arms, and the heat from the hundred candles started to melt the glue underneath my toupee. No kidding. Talk about a throw rug! I saw the tapes after the show, and you should have seen me struggle to hold on to the cake and to my store-bought hair with something resembling professional dignity. (Who knows, you're liable to see that clip turn up on one of those prime-time bloopers-and-blunders shows.) Now, whenever I'm wearing my ear-to-ear carpeting, I steer clear of birthday parties for anyone older than sweet sixteen!

The other "Today" show incident took place years before I arrived on the scene, but it's been passed on to me like an old family heirloom, so I'll just pass it along here. It seems that when the surgeon general's office first issued its warnings on cigarette packages in the early 1960s, someone at NBC thought it would be a good idea to find an oldster with a lifelong smoking history; leave it to a television newsman to play devil's advocate in these things. Well, somebody tracked down this one-hundred-year-old man from down south, and NBC flew him to New York to appear on the show the next morning. When the producer of the show finally met the old man and explained the idea behind the segment, the old man started to shake his head as if he couldn't deliver.

"You mean to tell me you want me to get up at seven o'clock in the morning and tell a national television audience I've been smoking two packs of cigarettes a day since I was twelve years old?" the old man asked, incredulous.

"That's right," the producer said. "That's the truth, isn't it?"

"Of course it's the truth," replied the old man. "The trouble is I don't stop coughing until eleven-thirty at the earliest."

I never fail to get a laugh with that one.

I am always happily astonished by the spit and pluck of some of the old folks I am lucky enough to meet, even though I've seen and heard enough to leave me way past the point of wonder. I look over at this little old lady seated in front of me on the Concorde, this fireball with the appetite of an army, as she fidgets with the cigar she had packed away in her purse, and I wouldn't trade my seat for anything in the world. (I won't tell you whether or not she lit up—I am, after all, a gentleman—but I will tell you this: I flew back the rest of the way with a smile on my face and a song in my heart.)

Let me close this little preamble with my own variation on a popular birthday toast: May you all live to be one hundred, and when you get there may mine be the loudest voice of congratulations you hear.

★ ★

Reba Kelley, the original pistol.

THE WHITE FOX

★ REBA KELLEY
Rochester, Minnesota

Reba Kelley is the original pistol. I can't think of a better way to describe her. She's got more energy than I do, this lady, and she's got about fifty years on me. She's 104 years old, this beautiful woman who is still something of a looker, and though she walks with a cane ("my stick," she calls it), she'd as likely whomp you over the head with the thing as she would use it to support herself.

We were first made aware of each other when Reba was living out in Marin County, California, accumulating something of a small fortune as a contestant on every television game show in town. Nice work, if you can get it. She even appeared on that ridiculous show Chuck Barris had on the air, "The Gong Show," and it tugs at my heart to say this, but Reba Kelley was gonged. Nobody, not even a panel of celebrity judges, respects their elders anymore.

"Oh, that was a lot of fun," Reba says when I remind her of her appearance. "I wanted to sing 'Old Pal,' but they told me it would be funnier if I sang 'The Old Gray Mare.' They

231

were right." Reba tells me proudly she turned over the $3,500 she received for the appearance to a friend and neighbor, who needed the money to outfit her son for the marines. "It went directly to her," she says. "Every time, when I would go on one of the shows, it would be for someone who needed the money. For a good cause, you know. All of them was for a purpose. I didn't want to keep the money for myself."

We didn't meet until much later, until Reba had moved to Minnesota for fear she would melt away in the California heat. "I was like a wilted rose out there," she recalls. "But I miss all of the good-looking men. I used to think, Oh, too bad I'm so old, I could teach these men a thing or two. That used to drive me crazy, I remember. Now at least I have peace of mind where that's concerned." I'm sure the good men of Rochester, Minnesota, will be happy to learn they're second-rate in Reba Kelley's book. "Oh, but they're sweet here, too," she says, covering herself. "It's just they're not hunks like out in California."

Reba lives now in a wonderful nursing facility called The Manor; it's part of the Bethany Samaritan Hospital out there, which does terrific work with the elderly. "Boy, we really bring 'em back from the dead out here," Reba boasts. "A lot of hospitals and old folks homes smell like smokestacks and booze joints, but not this place. It's sixty-five years old, this place, but it smells like it was just built."

Well, if The Manor doesn't smell like a smokestack or a booze joint, it's not for Reba Kelley's lack of trying. The last time I saw her she had a cigarette in one hand and a bourbon in the other. They call her "the White Fox" out at The Manor, partly for all the fuss and ruckus she manages to stir up and partly, I think, for the way she's able to outsmart pretty much everybody who comes in her path.

She's even got Ronald Reagan figured out better than any columnist or political analyst I've ever read or met: "He's too dramatic," she says, "and he doesn't think. Oh, he can memorize okay, but if he thinks he can pass that off as thinking, he better think again. He's got the two things, memorizing and thinking, all confused in his head." She reads the local newspaper every day, and she reads the *Wall Street Journal* and *Forbes* to stay on top of what's going on in the rest of the world; she reads George Will's column regularly, but she doesn't always agree with him. "He's a lot more brilliant than most people think," she says, and asks me if I'd seen the nasty way he's been treated recently by Jane's husband in the *Doonesbury* comic strip. (She's referring to cartoonist Gary Trudeau, who is married to my friend and "Today" show colleague Jane Pauley.) She doesn't miss a thing, this wonderful white fox of a woman.

Her secrets for a long life are quaint and sound: "Keep your meals simple and walk wherever you can," she preaches. "Also, if you can't sleep through the night, take catnaps during the day. That's the way a baby gets to outgrow its babyhood, and it's a good way to outgrow your adulthood, too." She drinks and smokes, but she says that since she turned one hundred she does both in moderation. "The doctors tell me I've got to take care of myself," she says.

Reba, who was born in Lamar, Missouri (Harry Truman was born on her mother's river-bottom farm), has let her long life take her to extended stopovers in all corners of the country. She even lived in midtown Manhattan, not far from the NBC studios, just after World War II, but the big city, she decided, wasn't for her. (Notice how it's not she who wasn't cut out for the big city.)

More than anything else, this good-looking white-haired pistol of a woman remembers the advent of the twin-engine plane as the most remarkable technological development of her lifetime. "Oh, I just couldn't believe how easy it was to fly," she says, remembering. "Everything else that's happened since then, the big fancy jets, everything else is just icing on the cake."

Her biggest joy in life comes from Mother Nature. "Flowers and trees," she says, "that's it for me. That is my life. I love the green of the garden, the way the flowers smell. July is my favorite time because everything then is in full bloom." But as summer turns to fall, Reba begins to worry about how her favorite plants and flowers will survive the winter. In October 1982, if you can believe it, she was actually arrested after Rochester police were tipped off to a little old lady stealing plants from a local liquor storefront. Actually, Reba wasn't actually arrested as much as she was nearly arrested; the police apologized when she explained she was only taking the plants home for the winter to preserve them for a spring replanting. The local papers dubbed Reba "the Flower Lady" shortly after the incident, and her landmark birthdays have since become a cause for local celebration.

That's about the time we first met, when all the local attention surrounding the flower incident came to my attention, when it finally occured to me that this feisty old broad and I should finally set up a how-dee-do. Boy, am I glad we finally got around to it.

Reba Kelley is in full bloom, even as she gets on in years, and I get the feeling that part of the reason she's lived such a long life is that she's taken time along the way to stop and smell and replant the flowers.

★ ★

THE KID NEXT DOOR

★ CHARLES EDWARD STROTHER
Delaplane, Virginia

We're cheating a little on this one, but what the heck. Mr. Charles Edward Strother isn't quite one hundred—he's but a spunky, young ninety-two-year-old—but he is my actual, honest-to-goodness neighbor down in Virginia, so I figured he ought to be included here.

Eddie Strother has always been a farmer, and he still is. As a matter of fact, Eddie used to farm and manage the land I'm living on now, so we do go back a number of years. Even at ninety-two, he is still active in the day-to-day operation of his 460-acre farm, although not quite as active as he would like. He also retains a seat on the board of directors of a local bank. "I've slowed down a little," he admits with a down-home honesty I've come to cherish and admire. "But you can't let yourself slow down too much, else what have you got? You've got to stay active in something. The worst thing an older person can possibly do is retire and just sit down. Work keeps you young."

Whatever it is, something has kept Eddie Strother going all these years, something's kept him young. The business of general farming has gotten generally easier in the years since he bought his first farm—he set himself up as a farmer when he returned from France after World War I—although the economics of the industry have always been hard to predict. "In those days it used to take eight or nine men to do what one man can do now," he calculates. "Let me tell you, if we had all the equipment then that we have today, we'd have had it easy. But I'm glad we had the hard work, the physical work. That kind of hard work keeps you young. When you work 'til you're exhausted, then you'll get a good night's sleep."

He's done a little bit of everything, my friend Eddie. He returned from the war as a sergeant, first class, in the medical corps, after which he was called on to do a little light doctoring for the good folks in and around his part of Virginia. He delivered a dozen babies and pulled more teeth than he cares to remember. During Prohibition, he set up a distillery with a childhood friend, and he started making his own apple-cider brandy and bourbon. Ah, now there's a man after my own heart (or after my liver, take your pick)! But the bourbon business wasn't quite booming—not for Eddie, anyway—and he and his partner soon sold out to a larger distillery.

Eddie used to live for hunting, and you should see his eyes light up when he talks about the sport that became one of his lifelong loves. "I raised hunters when I was younger," Eddie recalls, "and I was out there three or four times a week. Of course, that's the best way to train a hunter is out there in the middle of things, often as possible." (For those of you who don't get out much in hunting season, Eddie is talking about dogs here, and not folks, when he talks about training hunters.) General Patton was a frequent hunting partner of his in the late 1920s and early 1930s, and the two went after unsuspecting fox (or is it foxes?) like you wouldn't believe. "But now I've gotten too old for that," Eddie says sadly. "That's one of the things I miss."

Another sport that captured his lifelong fancy was our national pastime. Eddie stayed in France for a year after the war, asking for a transfer into one of our athletic companies stationed there, and he toured that country as a pitcher with a transplanted American baseball team. I would have loved to have seen him then—I'm told he was quite a pitcher—staring down the batters, giving them his best high heater. "I remember watching Walter Johnson, from the old Washington Senators," Eddie recalls. "He was some kind of pitcher. The players today, though, they're not the same. The entire game is just not the same. I can't believe it. In all athletics, not just baseball, the salaries have gotten out of all reason."

A lot of things have changed for Eddie since the horse-and-buggy days of his youth. "Your neighbors are just as far away now as they ever were," Eddie says, "but people in this day and time just don't know each other the way we did then. You'd think we'd all be more friendly now, what with the telephone and the automobile and everything, but nobody knows anybody anymore." You know, I listen to Eddie, and he's right; the two of us don't even get to see each other as often as we'd like, and our properties are adjacent to one another. I'm all over the map so much I hardly get to pop in on the folks next door. "In those days, we'd know everybody within a radius of eight or ten miles of home," he recalls fondly, with just a hint of loss in his voice. "Families were all here for a generation or two. Everybody knew everybody else, knew everybody else's business. It was nice."

These days, Eddie lives on his own. His wife lives in a nursing facility in nearby Fairfax, and he visits her whenever he can. (He's still able to drive, if you can believe it.) A cook comes in to help him with his meals a few days each week, but for the most part he fends for himself. As I mentioned earlier in this chapter, he still keeps active in his garden, and he grows all of his own vegetables—tomatoes, cantaloupes, beets . . . you name it, and my friend Eddie Strother has probably grown it at one time or another. "The general public never gets any fresh fruits or vegetables," Eddie says, "and nothing tastes sweeter than something you've grown yourself. Of course, part of that is because everything tastes better when you let it ripen on the vine. But a big part of it is the hands-on feeling, the idea that you've grown it yourself. I think that's true of most things you do, in the garden or anyplace else. Things mean more to you when you do it yourself."

Eddie has always been a do-it-yourself kind of guy, and I think that's one of the things that's kept him around and active and thriving all these years. He's also a think-for-yourself kind of guy, a quality he says is harder to come by today than ever before. "No, sir," he agrees, "that's one of the main things people don't do anymore. Probably one of the biggest changes I've seen in my lifetime. People don't think for themselves anymore, they let other people think for them. People now, everywhere, they get their opinions already formed from the news media, or from wherever, and that's a very dangerous thing. People just don't think. You've got to look at things, everything, from all sides, but most people only hear one side to every story, and they don't even bother to think things through. That's all they hear, and that's all they believe. There's two sides to every story, most times more, but people just don't think to look for them."

There are many sides to Eddie's story, but no matter how you look at it, he's a dear old friend. Everyone should be as lucky as I am to have a neighbor like him.

★ ★

THE DEAN OF DECATUR LAWYERS

★ THOMAS W. SAMUELS
Decatur, Illinois

We should all live as long and fruitful a life as Thomas W. Samuels, a gentleman and a scholar and by all accounts the oldest practicing lawyer in Decatur, Illinois. At the age of one hundred, he still works as a consultant with the Decatur

*"The ultimate luck was my choice of
ancestors."—Thomas W. Samuels.*

law firm that bears his name, and he meets once a week in
conference with the firm's partners and associates. "I'm not
as active as I used to be," T. W. admits, "but there are still a
few old clients who are under the illusion that I'm the only
one who knows the law."

They may be right. The law has changed considerably in
the more than seventy years since T. W., as his friends call
him, was awarded his law degree, and T. W. has learned to
change along with the times. He is a member of the American
Bar Association, the American Judicature Society, the American College of Trial Lawyers, and an honorary member of
the board of trustees of the University of Illinois, where he
received his education. He is also the author of a wonderful
book recalling his life and career called *Lawyer in Action*, a
copy of which now sits proudly in my library at home. "The
law today is much more complex and much more pervasive
in all society than it ever was," he asserts. "There is hardly a
business transaction conducted today that doesn't have significant tax and legal implications. It wasn't always that
way."

T. W. Samuels was born in a much simpler time and place.
The son of a home builder in Carrollton, Illinois, a small
town about twelve miles east of the Illinois River, T. W.

had a childhood that seems more than a century removed from today's fast-paced world. The biggest excitement, to hear T. W. tell it, was in meeting the "seven o'clock" train from St. Louis each evening. "Half the town came to see it," he recalls. On Decoration Day, the town's Civil War veterans would don their worn blue uniforms, unfurl their battle flags, and march through the town square preceded by the Carrollton Cornet Band. To me these days sound like something out of a history book, but to T. W. they are the wonderful stuff of childhood memories.

T. W. likes to muse over what he calls "those wonderful simple joys of boyhood, of going barefoot all summer, swimming in the creek south of town, sledding down snowy slopes, soaping windows on Halloween nights, shooting pigeons with my prized slingshot, hooking a ride on the rear end of the local ice wagon." His voice trails off wistfully as he looks out the window, gathering his thoughts. "All those wonderful days of long ago," he says softly, "forever gone except in the memory and dreams of an old man."

"A lot has changed since those days," T. W. says, pointing to the inventions and widespread availability of electricity, telephones, radios, cars, television, and, now, computers as the biggest innovators of that change. "I think I was most impressed by all of the wonderful advances in science," he muses, predicting that we'll soon see cures for cancer, diabetes, Alzheimer's disease, AIDS, and arthritis. "But after a while you take all of these developments in stride," he says.

His stride has slowed in recent years (he walks with a cane, and he has a wheelchair which he rarely uses), but nothing has stemmed his thirst for knowledge. In his early nineties he registered at Millikin University and took courses in philosophy, religion, and the history and appreciation of music. He guesses he's read about two books a week for the past fifteen years. "I read everything," he says, "romance, history, philosophy, and the *Wall Street Journal*. Every day." He recently told a local newspaper reporter that in reading so much he's beginning to find out how little he knows, a nice thought coming from a man of his years and achievements.

But T. W. knows enough not to worry about his weakening legs. "That's where all of the great athletes feel it first," he explains with a smile. Actually, T. W. was an avid tennis player throughout his adult life, until he gave up the sport for the less strenuous pursuit of golf, which he played into his middle eighties. "But now I've given up golf, and I've given up jogging. The last time I jogged I would say I was eighty-eight, maybe eighty-nine," T. W. figures, jogging his memory. "But of course that last time I only managed about a block or two." He laughs. Exercise now consists of daily leg lifts and light aerobics in his room at the Decatur Club, where he has lived for the past thirteen years.

Part of the reason T. W. has lived to such a ripe old age is in his genes—both his parents and his sister lived well into their nineties, and a grandfather lived to see his ninety-ninth birthday. "That's undoubtedly a factor," he guesses, "but I've also taken pretty good care of myself. If I'd known I'd have lived this long, maybe I would have taken even better care of myself." He eats, drinks, and smokes in moderation, and he still enjoys an occasional smoke throughout the day and a cocktail before dinner each evening. "I've been lucky all my life," T. W. says with a dry wit I'd come to look forward to during our meeting. "I've never been in a car crash, a falling plane, shot at, badly hurt or crippled, or suffered any serious illness. The ultimate luck, though, was in my choice of ancestors.

"I've always had a very positive view of life," T. W. says, "and I think that's helpful, too. There is no question of the power of the mind over the body. I'm impelled by that view. Every morning I tell myself I have a choice today. I can be happy or unhappy. I've always chosen to be happy, and I must say it's worked very well for me."

With 100 birthdays under his belt, number 101 doesn't get T. W. all that excited. "After you've had one hundred birthdays, they become rather routine," T. W. admits. "The golden years are not all they're cracked up to be. But seriously, I do approach each birthday now with a deep sense of gratitude and humility. I am grateful for God's grace, and for the many friends I've had, and humble as I perceive my insignificance in the cosmic context." As he begins his second century on this earth, he is anxious for what lies ahead.

"I'd like to live another one hundred years," he says, "because I'd like to see how history turns out."

History is important to T. W., and over his long and distinguished career he's seen a great deal of it in the making. He has lived through our efforts in five wars (the Spanish-American, World Wars I and II, and the Korean and Vietnam wars). He has crossed paths with former Presidents William Howard Taft and Richard Nixon, Chief Justices of the United States Supreme Court Earl Warren and Charles Evans Hughes, and Queen Elizabeth. "We were at a meeting of the American Bar in London in 1957, I think it was," he recalls, "and Queen Elizabeth invited me and some other lawyers to a garden party at Buckingham Palace. She was dignified and regal and altogether charming, but I remembered thinking about my first visit to the palace, in 1910, just after college. I stood outside the gates, just as the other tourists did, watching the changing of the guard, not dreaming that someday I'd be invited back as a guest of the queen."

One of his most memorable cases concerned the liability of a company that manufactured a tainted batch of soy sauce, the ingredients of which had been transported in a tank car that had previously been used to move a large shipment of a weed killer made with arsenic. T. W. hired a New Jersey firm to assist him in the case, and he worked closely with a young New Jersey lawyer from that firm for over a month. "I remember thinking at the time that this young man would go far," says T. W. "I was very impressed with his diligence." When, several years later, T. W. saw a young man named William J. Brennan appointed to the Supreme Court, his first impressions were borne out on the highest level.

T. W. even had the good fortune to argue a case himself before the United States Supreme Court, but that, he says, was nothing compared to the thrill of arguing (and winning) his first case as a young man in 1914. "To me that was, and in a sense still is, the most important case I ever tried," T. W. says—strong words coming from a man with approximately seventy years of trial experience. The case involved a claim of six dollars in wages. "I worked hard and prepared diligently," recalls T. W. "No victory in any other case has matched the sheer joy and triumph that I felt. That was the greatest thrill of my entire legal career."

In T. W.'s estimation, the legal profession has developed a poor public image over the past quarter century, partially, he says, "because of the greed and the lack of standards on the part of a few. The great bulk of lawyers today are still honest, and they maintain high ethical and moral standards.

"The law, apart from those who practice it, is the bulwark of the Republic," T. W. says proudly. "We have grown great and prosperous as a nation, and we have done it not by window bashing, flag waving, bomb throwing, or rampaging in the streets, but by legal means. The law, whether observed or broken, is the backbone of every civilized society. The only alternative to law is chaos."

In a life full of accomplishments, T. W. is proudest of his long marriage to his wife, Pauline (she died in 1973, nearly sixty years after they were married), and the two sons produced out of that union—William J., a retired airlines captain in Menlo Park, California, and Thomas W., Jr., a Decatur surgeon.

He is also proud of the way he has lived his life, and rightly so: "My deepest conviction, as I approach the end of a long life, is that truth and integrity are the only real and durable satisfactions of life, and that true success, not wealth or fame, comes only to the man who has attained the respect and to some degree the affection of those who know him through and through."

I'll second that emotion.

★ ★

AND THEN THERE'S MAUDE

★ MAUDE FISHER

Gladstone, Oregon

Maude Fisher is one of those grand and golden oldsters who come to me over the transom, one of the hidden trea-

"There's no doubt about it, dancing keeps you young."—Maude Fisher.

sures I find every day in my morning mail. I collect stories like Maude's, stories of triumph and perseverance and pluck, and hers stands nicely as representative of them all.

Not too long ago, Maude's daughter wrote asking me to celebrate her mother's 101st birthday on the air, which I was happily obliged to do, and I was so impressed with this dear old lady and her youthful spirit and energy that I thought I'd introduce you to her in these pages. She is typical of the quiet old gems I'm lucky enough to meet through this new on-air hobby of mine.

This dynamite little lady loves to dance, and she's got a growing collection of dance competition trophies to prove it. I'm told it's the dancing, more than anything else, that's kept her feeling light and lively in her later years. When I asked her how her dancing shoes were faring, she replied, "My dancing shoes are all right, but I don't think my feet are too good." She laughed right along with me at her own joke, then explained that she recently suffered a minor fall and would be off her feet for a few days before once again kicking up her heels in earnest.

"There's no doubt about it, dancing keeps you young," she insists. "There's nothing else like it. It keeps you on your toes, and it keeps your mobility up. People should dance more. If I didn't have the dancing to go to, I'd be in a rocking chair somewhere, not doing much of anything. I'll probably be dancing just as long as I live." Maude dances every Saturday night at her local senior center and in between whenever and wherever she can find some music, a willing partner, and a dance floor. Used to be she'd dance around her apartment doing housework, but she gave that up when she had the place carpeted. "Carpets are no good for dancing," she says, and you know, she's right about that.

Try as it might, age hasn't slowed down this incredible woman much at all. Even over the long-distance telephone, her wit and tongue seem as sharp as they could ever have been, and if she's aged at all, she's done so like a fine wine more than anything else. I've had less successful conversations with people half my age on the telephone; when she gets going full steam, as she does when a subject grabs her interest, I've got to race to keep up with her. Her memory is right on the money, and she has much to remember.

Maude's lessons for a long life are simple and to the point. "Never stuff yourself, and never hold a grudge," she says, one of my favorite answers to one of my favorite questions. "Other than that," she adds, "you're pretty much on your own." Words to live by, I suppose.

She's lived most all of her long life in the Pacific Northwest, and lately she's been living on her own in a small apartment in a Portland suburb. She lives there against the wishes and advice of her children and grandchildren, but really, she wouldn't have it any other way. "I don't feel old, I don't feel sick, and I don't feel tired," she says. "Why shouldn't I live by myself?" Maude has some trouble with her eyesight (she can't see well enough to read), and she sometimes has to walk with the aid of a cane, but other than these minor difficulties she says she is in fine fettle. She doesn't cook as much as she used to, or as much as she'd like, but that's okay with her. On her ninety-ninth birthday, Maude told a local newspaper reporter she felt as good as she did as a young woman of twenty-nine. "But now I don't feel quite that young anymore," she admits, "not as young as twenty-nine, anyway. Just say that I don't feel like I'm a hundred and one." Okay.

She's an avid basketball fan, Maude Fisher, and she never misses a Portland Trail Blazers game on the radio. Until recently, the city hosted a triple-A baseball team for many years, and she listened to all of their games as well. Her children tell me she's got the radio on full blast all the time, partly to keep her company and partly to serve as a substitute for the newspapers she can no longer read; they figure she'd be hard-pressed to find a roommate to put up with the racket.

The mother of six and the grandmother of nearly forty (she's lost count, she confesses), Maude is also the great-great-grandmother of six. "The way I'm going, I'll be a great-great-great-grandmother before too long," she says, laughing, and doesn't sound too displeased at the prospect. But though she's the matriarch of a large and growing family, Maude says she doesn't get to see her children and her children's children as often as she'd like. Like many families, hers is scattered across the country, and this, she says, is one of her deepest regrets these days.

From the looks of things, this terrific lady figures to be dancing up a storm for years to come. When I spoke to her last, she planned to enter yet another dance contest as soon as she was back on her feet from her untimely fall. She likes the people she meets at the senior center—her lifelong dance partners—and they like her just fine. "They promised to give me a big birthday party every year for as long as I live," she announces proudly. "And you know, if they leave it up to me, they just might regret that they ever made that promise. I'll be around for a while, and I'll hold them to it."

You can bet she will.

I tip my top hat and tails to this lovely lady and to all of the Maude Fishers of this world. Stick around, all of you; the world is a much richer place for your being here.

WHENEVER I meet someone who is getting up there in years, I ask two questions. The first thing I want to know is what single development in their long years has made the biggest difference in their day-to-day lives. Electricity scores high on everyone's list, as does the invention of the car, the telephone, the airplane, and the television (let's hear it for the television!).

But my favorite answer came from a one-hundred-year-old lady in Joplin, Missouri, who told me her life hasn't been the same since the arrival of R.F.D. mail: "We used to make a big trip to the post office with the whole family, first once a month or so and then once, maybe twice a week," she said. "Now I still can't believe it when somebody drives up to my door and puts my mail in my box. It happens every day, and I just can't get over it." It's the little things, really, that make a difference in the way we work and live.

The second thing I ask is their philosophy of life, their secrets of longevity. I think everybody wants to know how these folks have managed to string together such a long life. So again, in the interests of social science, I've compiled a list of the ten most common answers to my most common question. People live long because:

1. they've never smoked a cigarette in their life.
2. they've smoked a pack of cigarettes every day.
3. they go to church regularly.
4. they've never been to church.
5. they stay away from fried foods.
6. they eat nothing but fried foods.
7. they exercise regularly.
8. they never lift a muscle.
9. they've lived hard lives.
10. they've lived easy lives.

Seriously, a lot of people with fancy titles and fancy research grants have looked at the factors contributing to old age, and their results match pretty closely with mine. What I've found, first of all, is that old age tends to run in the family; for every 110-year-old-lady I've met, there's been a 90-year-old son waiting for her to cook his dinner. (I rest my case on this one with T. W. Samuels, the 100-year-old lawyer from Decatur, Illinois, you met earlier, whose parents and sister all lived well into their nineties.)

But that's a small point. Every single centenarian, and everyone with a shot at reaching that milestone, to a person, is easygoing. They hang in there, live life one day at a time, put one foot in front of the other, play it by ear, roll with the punches, keep on truckin', take life as it comes. Without exception, the gloriously old in our country are calm in nature, and they've been that way for most of their adult lives. They've learned to accept the cards they've been dealt, to control the things in their lives they have control over, and they don't lose any sleep over the things they can't control. I think we can all learn from that.

When I started out in this thing, many of the old folks I met were born during Abraham Lincoln's lifetime, so I checked to see if Honest Abe had anything to say about old age. He did: "The test of a people is how it behaves toward their own," he once said. "It is easy to love children. Even tyrants and dictators make a point of being fond of children. But the affection and care for the old, the incurable, the helpless, are true gold mines of a culture."

And I am proud to be one of many to help lead the gold rush.

14 Hold That Thought

So there you have it, a brisk little walk through my American neighborhood. Not a bad place to live and work, if I do say so myself. I've put down roots here, and I'm happy as a prize-winning pig that I did.

I wouldn't want to live any other way, in any other place or time, even though I must confess to an occasional craving for days gone by when life was much simpler and we all minded everybody else's business as much as we minded our own. Sometimes I miss the "good old days" when we all had the time to wave to folks as we crossed the street, to spin a yarn or two over the backyard fence, and to get wind of little snippets of town gossip like old Sadie Mae next door chipping her tooth on an apple week before last. Now that everything's become faster and more convenient, we've all grown a lot more private, and this big busybody sometimes hankers after that certain sense of community, of belonging to a much larger whole. That's why I love to travel around this glorious country of ours to say howdy and pass the time of day with as many folks as I can. It reinforces my long held belief that the best thing America has got going for her is her people.

This is a country made up of neighborhoods like yours and mine. We are the sum of our parts—and our parts, our neighbors, are all kinds of special. These are my neighbors, the folks you've met in the preceding pages, and I've collected their stories and their friendships over the years to help make my world seem smaller, more intimate, more manageable. With a schedule like mine, going all over the place and back again, things can get out of hand, the world can suddenly seem like too much to handle. But if you've got wonderful friends wherever you go, as I do, then it's easier to cope, to feel a part of things, connected. When I stop someplace, even if it's just for an hour or two between planes, I feel at home, like I belong, and I feel that way because of the great and good people you've met here, and others like them.

It's a swell neighborhood, my America, and I hope I never see the day when I have to move. I know, I know, I sound like a hokey broken record, but that's the way my friends around the country make me feel. Really. Truly.

Thanks for stopping by for a visit. I'll see you 'round the neighborhood!

Every effort has been made to establish the source of these photos. We will be glad to rectify any error or omission if we are notified of same.

★ ★

PHOTO CREDITS